SAINT
JOHN MASIAS

BOOKS BY MARY FABYAN WINDEATT

A Series of Twenty Books

Stories of the Saints for Young People ages 10 to 100

THE CHILDREN OF FATIMA
And Our Lady's Message to the World

THE CURÉ OF ARS
The Story of St. John Vianney, Patron Saint of Parish Priests

THE LITTLE FLOWER
The Story of St. Therese of the Child Jesus

PATRON SAINT OF FIRST COMMUNICANTS
The Story of Blessed Imelda Lambertini

THE MIRACULOUS MEDAL
The Story of Our Lady's Appearances to St. Catherine Labouré

ST. LOUIS DE MONTFORT
The Story of Our Lady's Slave, St. Louis Mary Grignion De Montfort

SAINT THOMAS AQUINAS
The Story of "The Dumb Ox"

SAINT CATHERINE OF SIENA
The Story of the Girl Who Saw Saints in the Sky

SAINT HYACINTH OF POLAND
The Story of the Apostle of the North

SAINT MARTIN DE PORRES
The Story of the Little Doctor of Lima, Peru

SAINT ROSE OF LIMA
The Story of the First Canonized Saint of the Americas

PAULINE JARICOT
Foundress of the Living Rosary & The Society for the Propagation of the Faith

SAINT DOMINIC
Preacher of the Hail Mary and Founder of the Dominican Order

SAINT PAUL THE APOSTLE
The Story of the Apostle to the Gentiles

SAINT BENEDICT
The Story of the Father of the Western Monks

KING DAVID AND HIS SONGS
A Story of the Psalms

SAINT MARGARET MARY
And the Promises of the Sacred Heart of Jesus

SAINT JOHN MASIAS
Marvelous Dominican Gatekeeper of Lima, Peru

SAINT FRANCIS SOLANO
Wonder-Worker of the New World and Apostle of Argentina and Peru

BLESSED MARIE OF NEW FRANCE
The Story of the First Missionary Sisters in Canada

SAINT JOHN MASIAS

MARVELOUS DOMINICAN GATEKEEPER OF LIMA, PERU

By
Mary Fabyan Windeatt

Illustrated by
Sister Mary of the Compassion, O.P.

TAN BOOKS AND PUBLISHERS, INC.
Rockford, Illinois 61105

Nihil Obstat: Arthur J. Scanlan, S.T.D.
                 Censor Librorum

Imprimatur: ✠ Francis J. Spellman, D.D.
                 Archbishop of New York
                 New York, July 25, 1944

This work first appeared, in serial form, under the title *Warrior in White: The Story of Blessed John Masias*, in the pages of *The Torch*. First published in book form, by Sheed & Ward, New York, in 1944.

ISBN: 0-89555-428-3

Library of Congress Catalog Card No.: 93-61382

Printed and bound in the United States of America.

TAN BOOKS AND PUBLISHERS, INC.
P.O. Box 424
Rockford, Illinois 61105

1993

For
Mother Mary of the Immaculate Heart, O.P.,
of the
Dominican Sisters of the Perpetual Rosary,
Union City, New Jersey.

CONTENTS

ACKNOWLEDGMENT

The author wishes to thank Reverend Norbert Georges, O.P., Director of the Blessed Martin Guild, for his help and encouragement in preparing this first English biography of Blessed [now Saint] John Masias.

SAINT
JOHN MASIAS

CHAPTER 1

SHEPHERD BOY

THE AFTERNOON sun was hot. It beat down on the dusty valley with such strength that the solitary traveler, making his way to the village of Rivera, paused for a moment to mop his brow.

"I'd better stop by that oak tree on the hill," he told himself. "There's no use going farther in this heat."

The oak, gnarled and immense, was the only sizeable tree in sight. It cast a huge shadow on the ground, and the traveler gratefully sank down upon the parched grass. His eyes rested but briefly on the dazzling white ribbon of a road that wound through the valley to Rivera. How tired he was! And how far away America seemed—the land of his dreams! Yet he knew that in a little while he would feel more cheerful. Already Madrid was behind him, and Cordoba. Next would come Seville and Cadiz. With luck, there would be a boat there to take him to Cartagena in the New World.

"Gold," murmured the traveler dreamily, "gold

and more gold in Peru! Pounds of gold! Tons of it, if a man is lucky!"

It was fairly comfortable in the shade of the old oak, and the traveler felt his eyes closing. In a little while he would be on his journey with fresh courage. Just now, though, it would be better to rest. So, with a deep sigh of exhaustion, the man stretched out upon the grass, his bundle under his head, and fell asleep.

Two hours later he stirred and unconsciously pulled his worn coat over his shoulders. The sun was moving toward the west and a little breeze had come up out of nowhere. It was cooler now, but the traveler still felt no urge to be on his way. He would sleep a little longer. Yet even as he settled himself once again, his ears caught a curious sound. Someone was talking, and quite near at hand. Rather, someone was praying. The words were familiar. *Hail Mary, full of grace, the Lord is with thee. . .blessed art thou amongst women. . .*

The traveler opened one eye and squinted at the valley below. A flock of sheep was spread out along the river banks. Turning away from the peaceful scene, the man suddenly gasped with astonishment. A few yards away a boy about ten years old was kneeling on the edge of a little embankment. The rays of the setting sun were on his upturned face, a poor wooden rosary in his hands, his shepherd's staff beside him.

Holy Mary, Mother of God, pray for us sinners now and at the hour of our death. Amen.

The boy's voice was clear as a bell. He gave no

sign that he was aware of being observed; the beads slipped through his young hands in a gentle rhythm. By now sleep had vanished from the traveler, and he stared with amazement at the boy before him. On his journey from the north of Spain he had seen many a shepherd lad, but none quite like this. Why, the youngster was as devout as though he prayed in a cathedral!

Presently the boy completed his rosary and placed the wooden beads in a scuffed leather satchel that hung from his shoulder. Then, picking up his wooden staff, he jumped lightly down the embankment. As he did so, a ragged white dog appeared from nowhere and ran eagerly after him.

"Wait a minute!" called the man. "Shepherd boy! Wait a minute!"

The sound hit the still air abruptly. The lad turned toward the embankment, the dog at his heels, and the traveler saw that he had an intelligent face, tanned by the sun and wind. And his dark eyes were friendly.

"Yes, sir? You're looking for the town?"

The man shook his head. "No, lad. I know the way to Rivera. But what were you doing a little while ago? Over there on your knees?"

The boy smiled faintly, while his fingers played with the dog's rough coat. "I was offering the Holy Rosary for the Souls in Purgatory."

"What?"

"I was praying for the Souls in Purgatory."

The man laughed. "But that's a work more suited for women than a likely lad of your years."

"Men and boys go to Purgatory, too, sir. It's well that all of us pray for them, that very soon they will be ready to see God in Heaven."

Something in the little shepherd's voice caused the man to stop his joking. "You'd make a good preacher, young friend. What's your name?"

"John Masias, sir, although really it is John d'Arcos. But my father is dead and I use my uncle's name."

The traveler nodded and began to fumble in a pocket. "Here," he said, bringing out a small silver coin, "take this and pray for me, too, John. I'm not a Soul in Purgatory, but I do have troubles."

The boy shook his head. "I think you need all your money, sir. You're on a trip, without a home or anyone to look after you."

"Take it, boy, in return for your prayers."

"But I pray without being paid!"

The man threw up his hands in amazement. "What a lad! Here—look at this coin. Is anything wrong with it?"

"No, sir."

"Then, in God's Name, do what I tell you! Take it and put it to some good use."

Slowly the young shepherd stretched out his hand. "All right," he said simply. "I'll pray very hard that you find happiness in America."

"*America*? What makes you think I'm going there?"

The boy laughed. "Most travelers are going to America these days. In a few years I am going, too."

The traveler nodded shrewdly. "Ah, so you're an

ambitious lad after all, in spite of your prayers! Well, America will have enough gold for both of us, I'm sure."

When the traveler had gone on his way, the young shepherd stood looking after him thoughtfully. Perhaps he should have explained his interest in America at greater length. He, poor orphan boy that he was, had no desire to obtain a fortune in gold or silver. He was going to the New World only because he felt it was God's Will.

"Why didn't I say so?" he wondered. "Too many people are going to America to take what they can for themselves. Hardly anyone is going just to be of use to the poor and ignorant."

He was lost in these thoughts when suddenly his keen ears caught the sound of someone scrambling up the hillside from the valley.

"That must be Mary," thought the boy. "But she's very late. I wonder why?"

By now the white sheep dog was barking excitedly, hidden from view by the bushes that screened the path leading to the oak tree. John seized his wooden staff and started down the hill. Was something wrong? The dog didn't usually bark like this when his little sister came to help him with the sheep.

"Here I am!" he called. "Over this way, Mary!"

The echo of his own voice filled the valley, but there was no reply. Quickly he pushed his way through the tangle of vines and bushes that hid the little path. Then he stopped. A seven-year-old girl, in the plain wool garb of a peasant child, was huddled on a stone a few yards away. And she was crying as though her heart would break.

The boy stared. "What's happened, Mary? What's the trouble?"

Slowly the child looked up at her brother, her little face strained and pale in its frame of long black braids. "Oh, John, I thought you'd gone away!" she choked between sobs. "I thought I'd never see you again! I wasn't even going to come here at first. . .and now I'm late, and we won't be able to get the sheep together before dark. . ."

The tears were falling again. "There, there," said the boy soothingly. "I've told you dozens of times that I won't go to America for a long time. Why can't you believe me?"

The child hid her face in her hands. "I don't see why you have to go at all," she whimpered.

The young shepherd sighed. This little sister was his closest living relative. Since the death of their parents, five years ago, the two of them had been living with a farmer down in the valley. They did odd jobs around the house and occasionally went to Rivera to see their uncle, a good man who regretted that he had no room for them in his own house. Actually, however, there was no one to give Mary the love and care every little girl should have.

John sat down on the stone and drew his small sister to him. "Listen," he whispered, taking her hand in his, "a traveler passed by a while ago and left you something. What do you suppose it is?"

For a moment Mary was silent. Then she peered timidly through tear-stained fingers. "What?"

"I THOUGHT YOU HAD GONE AWAY," SHE SAID.

The boy held out his hand. A ray of sunlight
stealing through the vines and bushes glistened on
the little silver coin. "Here," he said, "it's all yours."

Suddenly tears were a thing of the past. The
child reached for the coin eagerly, turning it over
and over to make sure it was real. It was the first
time she had ever held a piece of money in her
hand.

"Oh, John! The traveler must have been a very
nice man! Who was he?"

The boy shook his head. "I don't know. Someone
who asked our prayers that he would find happiness
where he was going."

"It wasn't...the vision again? Saint John the
Evangelist didn't give you this little coin?"

The young shepherd laughed. "No. It wasn't the
good saint who came this time. Just a poor man
on his way to America to make a fortune."

Mary sighed with relief. "I'm glad. You don't
know how it hurts when Saint John comes and says
God wants you to leave me."

"Mary! He doesn't put it that way!"

"What does he say then?"

The shepherd boy shifted uneasily. It was always
hard to explain just what happened when the vision
came. He would be watching the sheep, perhaps
saying the Rosary, when all of a sudden he would
know that his patron, John the Evangelist, was
beside him. The first vision had come to him over
five years ago, when he was just a tiny boy. Since
then there had been several others. Each time, the
holy Apostle brought the same message.

"What does he tell you, John?"

"He tells me I am to leave Spain and that some day churches will be built in my honor."

"He doesn't really say you'll travel to America."

"No, but I think I'm going there just the same."

"What else?"

John smiled faintly. "Many times my patron saint gives me a glimpse of a beautiful country. Everything is clean and shining and the people are so happy. I'm very sure it must be Heaven. Oh, Mary! If only you could see it, too!"

The little girl looked down at the silver coin in her hand. The old sadness was stealing over her. She never had any visions. And one of these days Saint John the Evangelist was going to take her brother away for good. What would she do then?

CHAPTER 2

THE JOURNEY

AS HE GREW older, John Masias worked hard
to provide for his young sister. He felt sure
that everything would turn out well and
that she would marry a good man when the time
came. Perhaps Mary's husband might even be
blessed with plenty of this world's goods. If so, then
John could go to America with a clear conscience.

"When will it be, Lord?" he often wondered.
"When do You want me to start working for You
in the New World?"

Alas! Such prayers always went unanswered, and
presently John came to realize that it was God's
Will for him to continue his shepherd's life. So he
followed the usual routine in the quiet hills near
Rivera. Each morning he drove his master's sheep
to pasture. Each night he brought them home
again. In the long hours between, he thought and
prayed. Three times a day he said the Rosary—once
for the Souls in Purgatory, once for sinners, once
for the extension of Christ's Kingdom throughout
the world. On the surface it was a dull life for a

SAINT JOHN THE EVANGELIST
HAD COME TO HIM AGAIN!

boy, but John did not complain. He was confident that someday truly great things would happen to him.

One bright summer morning in the year 1665, when John was twenty years old, he took his flocks as usual to graze in the hills. When they were dispersed, he settled himself by the old oak tree and looked out at the valley. He was happy today. There was a feeling of real peace in his heart. What did it matter if he had to spend his whole life as a shepherd, never leaving his native Spain?

"Doing what God wants me to do is the only thing that matters," he thought. "That's all I have to remember."

Suddenly a hand was laid gently upon his shoulder. John looked up, and then his heart gave a great leap of joy at the vision before him. Through the mercy of God, Saint John the Evangelist, his friend and patron, had come to him again!

At once the youth knelt down, marveling at the glorious vision. It was one of many granted to him since childhood. The saint was clothed in a white robe and seemed to be about John's own age. His face was wonderfully kind and shone with an unearthly radiance.

"Peace be to you, little brother," he said kindly. "Are you ready to go on a journey?"

The eyes of the shepherd boy were bright with excitement. "Oh, yes!" he cried.

Saint John nodded. "You have served God faithfully for twenty years in the simple way He desired for you. Now you are to serve Him in great ways."

From a distance came the faint bleating of sheep. A flock of crows, their black wings glistening in the sun, swooped overhead in noisy flight. The air was alive with the many sounds and scents of spring-time, but John Masias heard and felt nothing of these. His eyes were fixed with affectionate wonder upon his friend and patron. Here was one of the twelve Apostles, the beloved disciple of Our Lord! What a marvelous grace that God should set aside the laws of nature and allow John the Evangelist to guide and comfort him!

"Tell me what to do, good saint," he said simply. "Remember, I am just a poor country boy."

The Apostle smiled again. "Take my hand. We shall make this trip together."

Holding fast to his heavenly friend, John Masias presently found himself traveling the dusty road that led to Guadalcanar. In some mysterious fashion he seemed to move with amazing speed. It was like skimming over the ground, as though his feet had wings. Soon Rivera was far behind and the familiar scenes of childhood. Surely America lay ahead— the land of savages who knew not Christ, whose mountains abounded in gold and precious gems!

Suddenly the young shepherd turned to his patron anxiously. "Good saint, I forgot to say good-bye to my sister! And the sheep. . . I left them alone in the hills!"

Upon hearing John's anxious words the Apostle nodded. "Don't worry," he said. "The Queen of Heaven will watch over your sister, and I shall attend to the sheep. But right now, little brother,

I am going to take you to my own country. Look!"

Suddenly the rolling Spanish hills were no more—the olive groves, the stretching miles of trees with their golden burden of oranges. Instead, the young man's astonished eyes beheld a shining city, filled with angels and saints. Sweet music sounded in his ears. John the Evangelist, as he had done several times before, was giving his young namesake a glimpse of Heaven!

"This is your true home," said a voice deep in his heart. "Here is the only happiness that lasts, John. Look and remember!"

How the wonder was accomplished the young shepherd did not know. Had he actually been taken to Heaven? Or was it with the eyes of the soul that he saw such splendor? There was no way of telling. But the young man's heart was filled with sorrow as the beautiful vision faded away, leaving him in the everyday world again. A lump came into his throat as he realized that as yet he had not the right to enjoy the happiness of the saints. How drab everything seemed, despite the loveliness of trees and sky! How empty! Then genuine dread filled his heart as he looked about. He did not recognize the countryside! And his patron saint was no longer visible!

"Please come back!" he cried. "Good saint, don't leave me alone again!"

There was no reply. Although John strained his eyes, peering this way and that, he could catch no glimpse of his friend's white robe. This was a terrible disappointment, but to make matters worse he could see that a bad storm was brewing. Angry clouds were piling up in the western sky. Throughout the ominous mass streaked fiery fingers of light. On all sides the boughs of the orange and olive trees tossed in the growing wind.

John shivered. A short time ago he had been so happy. The good Apostle had said the time had come for him to do great things for God. The quiet days of being a shepherd were over at last. But wasn't it better to be a shepherd at Rivera, among friends and good neighbors, than to be adrift on a lonely road in a storm?

"Where am I?" he cried, knowing full well there was no one to hear or care. Then, as a mighty burst of thunder rent the heavens, he remembered the abiding presence of God within his soul. "I trust in You, Lord," he said. "It really doesn't matter where I am as long as You are in my heart."

It was fortunate that an abandoned hut stood close by. As the first drops of rain spattered down on the dusty road, John ran toward it eagerly. It was a musty little place, with only one window and a door that sagged on rusty hinges. But the roof was surprisingly good, and John remained warm and dry while the storm raged out-of-doors. He even managed to take a short sleep, during which he dreamed that he was in far-away Peru. Diamonds and emeralds lay about on the ground, to be had for the taking. He picked up huge quantities of these and sold them at a good price. Then he gave a great banquet for all the needy he could find. These poor souls, their natural hunger satis-

fied, listened eagerly as he told them of God, His
Commandments, His Church. Many asked to be
baptized, so that someday they could go to Heaven,
too. Presently the air was echoing with one cry:
"Help us, John Masias! Teach us what is right!"
When he finally awoke from this strange dream,
the black clouds had rolled away. A gorgeous rain-
bow stretched across the western sky and the clean,
cool air was filled with the song of birds. As the
young shepherd made his way back to the road, he
noted a weatherbeaten signpost. It was fashioned
in the shape of an arrow and bore one word:
SEVILLE.

"So this is where I am going!" he thought. "Dear
Saint John, why didn't you tell me?"

As he continued to walk along, picking his way
through the puddles, John found his rosary and
began the familiar task of offering this favorite
prayer to the Queen of Heaven. He was thus
engaged when he noted a figure coming toward
him. The stranger was a tall, well-built man and
wore the rough clothes of a farmer. He was leading
a little donkey which looked even smaller under its
load of fruit and vegetables.

As the newcomer approached, he cast a shrewd
glance at the young shepherd. "You're looking for
work?" he asked hopefully.

John shook his head. "I am going to Seville, sir.
After that, I hope to make my way to the sea and
take passage on a boat for America."

The farmer snorted. "America! Every young fool
is going there! Listen to me, friend. You'd be wiser

to stay in Spain and not lose your health trying to
find gold in some wild jungle. As for me, I'll give
you an honest wage, good food and lodgings, if
you'll help out on my farm. What do you say?"

John smiled. "Thank you, sir, but I think I ought
to get to Seville as soon as I can."

"I suppose farming isn't good enough for you?"

"It's not that, sir. I just feel. . ."

"Nonsense! Don't try to explain. All young men
are the same. They want money, excitement, travel.
They're fools, all of them. The only decent kind of
life is on the land, young friend. Believe me!"

For a moment the young shepherd stood with
downcast eyes, quietly rubbing the donkey's ears.
Then, as though a problem had been settled, he
looked up at the farmer. "You're worried about
something," he said kindly.

"Worried? Of course I'm worried. Last month
my two boys went off to America—the wretches!
My wife tripped over a stone and hurt her leg. Now
there's no one to do the farm chores but me. It's
too much, I tell you. In a year I'll be in a grave
from overwork."

John laughed. "Don't feel too bad," he said.
"Maybe I could come and help you for a little
while."

An expression of amazement crossed the farmer's
face, followed quickly by a glimmer of hope. "You
mean it, young man? You're not just fooling?"

"I'm not fooling, sir. I'll do my best to be of use."

"Then God be praised!" cried the farmer. "You
can come along with me to Guadalcanar right now.

Of course it's rather late to be taking things to market, but there's a fair going on and the fruit and vegetables will sell well even at night."

So John seized the donkey's rope bridle and began to retrace his steps. He was puzzled and amused at the sudden turn of events. The words Saint John had spoken to him that morning still sounded in his heart: *"You have served God faithfully for twenty years, in the simple way He desired for you. Now you are to serve Him in great ways."* Of course these words were still true, but in what a strange way the saint worked to make them so! He caused a poor shepherd boy to travel untold miles in a miraculous manner, gave him a glimpse of Heaven, then apparently abandoned him in a strange corner of Spain!

"May the Will of God be done!" said John softly.

The farmer looked up. "What's that, young friend? What did you say?"

John smiled. "It was just a prayer, sir. A very little prayer."

CHAPTER 3

INCIDENT IN SEVILLE

JOHN REMAINED with his new-found friend for several weeks, making himself useful in many ways. The farmer and his wife were delighted, for they found the young man an excellent worker. The crops were prospering under his care and the cattle thriving as never before.

"I'm convinced that the boy's a saint," the woman told her husband one day. "Ever since you brought him here, I've had no more trouble with my leg. Really, it's simply wonderful the way his prayers for my health were answered!"

"It is," said the farmer. "I only wish I could pay the lad what he's worth."

John was happy on the farm, however, and never dreamed of asking for more wages. Yet all the same he felt that this quiet life would not last much longer. Deep in his heart there was a conviction that God still wished him to go to Seville.

"And after that to America," the boy told himself. "Dear Lord, it is in America that You want me to work, isn't it?"

Sometimes the familiar question was answered by a deep feeling of inner peace. At others, there was only emptiness. John did his best to accept such trials, however, and not a day passed that he did not ask for an increase in faith. With faith in God, all things are easy. Doing His Will, even when it means just waiting, becomes the most satisfying thing in the world.

One night, after a hard day's labor in the fields, John was awakened from sleep. He sat up in bed and looked around. All of a sudden the plain little room was filled with a strange light. It played upon the cracked walls, the old chair and table by the window, then came to rest upon the boy's uplifted face. Quickly he stretched out his arms toward the heavenly radiance.

"Saint John!" he breathed softly. "Is it you again?"

There was a slight pause, and then came the voice he had learned to love. "Yes, little brother. But hurry now. The time has come to make another journey."

John jumped out of bed. In five minutes he was ready, his few possessions packed neatly in a blanket the farmer's wife had given him.

"Seville!" he cried eagerly. "Do we go to the city at last?"

The heavenly radiance grew brighter, and presently the young man's eyes rested on a familiar figure in the midst of the light. Saint John the Evangelist, in garments white as snow, was smiling at him and nodding his head.

"We go to Seville," he said. "Come—give me your hand."

Then, as had happened so often before, the shepherd lad of Rivera found himself transported through the air with wonderful speed. The farm, the little room that had been home to him for so many weeks, the familiar sights and sounds of the country, were gone. Then suddenly he came to himself. He was alone, wandering down a broad and busy avenue in the city of Seville.

As he had learned to do on previous occasions, the youth stifled his disappointment at being separated from his beloved patron saint. After all, it must be God's Will that he find his way about the city alone. The holy Apostle could not be with him all the time. So, with a little prayer for guidance, he set himself to enjoy the new scenes about him.

Great buildings arose on every side—churches and palaces and shops. And though it was still early in the morning, the street was crowded. Men passed by, dressed in rich velvet and silk, their fine steel swords clanking as they walked. An occasional carriage rumbled through the street in the direction of the Cathedral, and John caught glimpses of women, their faces hidden by heavy veils, on their way to early Mass. Here and there sidewalk merchants were setting up stands for the day and crying out the merits of their wares in loud voices.

The young man looked about with interest. Seville! What a crowded place it was! And how busy everyone seemed! Never had he seen so many people at once.

"You, there!" cried a voice suddenly. "Do you want to earn an honest penny?"

John stopped. A swarthy, middle-aged man, obviously in charge of a pastry stand, was beckoning to him. The stranger was short but powerfully built, and his eyes, as they glanced quickly at the young shepherd's country garb, were crafty.

"You called me, sir?"

"That's right. I need someone to look after my stand for an hour. You've got an honest face. What do you say?"

John looked at the stranger, then at the piles of little cakes stacked before him on the counter, the long golden loaves. "Of course I'll help you," he said with a friendly smile. "Yours is a good trade. What do you want me to do?"

The merchant chuckled. "Just watch this place while I'm gone. If anyone wants to buy, the cakes are a penny each and the loaves two pennies. But don't let anyone try to cheat you."

"Cheat me, sir? Why should anyone want to do that?"

"Seville is full of rascals, young friend from the country. But don't worry too much. I'll be back in an hour and then you can go about your own business."

John nodded, a bit puzzled. There was something peculiar about the merchant. Why, for instance, should he be so anxious to leave his pastry stand in charge of a complete stranger?

"I guess it's all right," John told himself finally. "I'm not used to the ways of city folk, that's all."

The minutes passed and the shepherd boy made several sales. But though he himself was hungry, having missed his breakfast at the farm, he touched none of the tempting wares before him. Possibly the merchant would let him have a loaf or two when he returned.

"Only last week I sent all my wages to Mary," he thought. "If I did have a few pennies now, how fine it would be to buy some of this bread!"

Presently the bells in a nearby church tower pealed seven times. John looked down the street. The hour was up. The merchant should be returning at any moment. But the merchant did not return. Another hour passed, then two, and still there was no sign of him. By now, one-third of the cakes and bread was sold, and John decided to arrange the rest more attractively. Busy with this task, he did not see the small boy approach who seemed to appear from nowhere, a large sack in his hand, but he heard his shout. With a skill born of long practice, the child began to scoop cakes and bread into the sack. Almost in the same instant a second and larger boy jumped on John from behind and knocked him to the ground.

"Help!" John cried. "Don't steal these things! They're not mine!"

"Who cares?" laughed the boys. "We're hungry!"

No one in the crowded street seemed to notice what was taking place, and when John finally picked himself up from the ground, the agile young thieves had disappeared. And they had taken not only the remaining cakes and bread but the money from the morning's sales.

"What am I going to do?" cried John. "How can I explain to the merchant?"

The words were no sooner out than the young shepherd's heart sank still farther. Coming down the street was the owner of the pastry stand. He was walking very fast and seemed to be excited.

"I never meant to be gone this long!" he told John breathlessly. "Oh, my dear young friend, how I've imposed upon you! Please accept my apologies!"

John was silent, his eyes upon the empty counter. The merchant followed his gaze, then gave him a reassuring clap on the back.

"But you've sold everything! Why, that's splendid, young friend! Splendid! Now it's my turn to be of use. I'm going to repay you for your fine help."

John took a deep breath and shook his head. "I was robbed while you were away, sir. The cakes and bread are gone. The money, too. Oh, if I could tell you how bad I feel..."

The merchant stared, and his crafty eyes lit up with a dangerous fire. "*You were robbed?*"

"Yes, sir. Only two minutes ago. Some boys came and set upon me without the least warning."

The man stiffened. All his friendliness was gone now, and he seized John in a merciless grip. "You lie!" he roared. "Give back what you took! No young man from the country can make a fool out of me!"

In vain John tried to plead his cause. The merchant would not listen, but rained blows upon him.

"IT'S FATHER PETER!" THEY WHISPERED
FEARFULLY. "RUN, EVERYBODY!"

An eager crowd gathered in front of the little stand, laughing and shouting at the prospect of a fight. Two men took the young shepherd's bundle, and soon his few belongings were scattered on the street.

"He's hidden the money somewhere!" cried one. "Let's see who finds it first!"

"The wretched thief!" put in another. "This will teach him to trick an honest merchant!"

The hubbub continued. John, now bruised and bleeding, felt sure that his hour had come. He was no match at all for the angry owner of the pastry stand. Yet suddenly the shouts died away and an uneasy hush fell upon the little gathering. A priest had appeared, clad in the black and white habit of the Dominican Order, and he was viewing the little scene with a stern eye.

"It's Father Peter!" whispered someone fearfully. "Run, everybody!"

At once the merchant relaxed his merciless grip and slipped away into the crowd. John looked up, his face covered with dust and blood, and the eyes of the strange priest met his own with a look of compassion.

"Father. . .I didn't mean to lose. . .the money!" stammered John. "The two boys. . .before I could do anything. . ."

"Don't try to talk," said the priest kindly. Then, staring the crowd in the face, he drew himself up to his full height.

"Get back to your work!" he roared. "And ask God to have mercy on your souls!"

The crowd obeyed rapidly, for Father Peter was not a man with whom anyone trifled. He possessed great physical strength, and all Seville knew that he allowed no injustice toward the poor or sick. Indeed, his sermons at the Dominican church had made many a sinner tremble with fear and return to the Sacraments with undreamed-of haste.

Not knowing quite what he did, John took the helping hand the friar extended and rose unsteadily to his feet. Then, in sudden despair, he realized that his bundle was gone. The few possessions he had in the world were now in the hands of others!

"Don't worry," said the priest kindly, reading his anxious thoughts. "We'll go to the Dominican convent and you can tell me all about everything— although I believe I have a fair idea even now."

"Yes, Father," whispered John weakly.

Later in the day, after a good meal and a change of clothes, the young shepherd felt much better. He could even be a little amused at Father Peter's insistence that the two boys who had robbed him were none other than the merchant's own sons.

"They've done it before," said the friar dryly, "although this time they didn't pick the right person."

John shook his head. "I don't understand, Father."

"Probably not. But the previous victims of this little trick were also travelers, John—men on their way to America with all their wealth in a pack like yours. They settled their accounts with the merchant by giving him everything they owned."

"And I had nothing!"

"Precisely. That's why the man was so angry. Ah, my son, Seville is no place for you! You're a country boy at heart. You don't know the ways of city thieves and rascals."

John smiled. "I never really wanted to live here," he said shyly. "You see, Father, I have an idea that God wants me to do some work for Him in America —perhaps among the poor and sick."

The friar was quiet a moment, shrewdly observing his young guest. Finally he spoke, slowly and clearly.

"I think you'd be better off in some country place in Spain. And you'll do me a favor if you go to one little town in particular."

"Where, Father?"

"To Jerez de la Frontera. Do you know where it is?"

The young man nodded. "It's not far from Seville. But why should I go there, Father?"

The priest smiled. "I have an idea you'll soon find out. Look—I'm going to give you a letter to the Father Prior there. You see, John, it hasn't taken me long to discover one thing. In my opinion you have a religious vocation. I think you'd be very happy as a Dominican friar."

The young shepherd stared. "But I want to go to America, Father Peter!"

The priest smiled again. "Have a talk with the Father Prior first, then make up your mind. You will, won't you, as a favor to me?"

John was silent a moment. Then his eyes brightened. The Will of God! Sometimes it made itself clear in the strangest ways!

"All right," he said eagerly. "I'll go, Father Peter."

CHAPTER 4

WESTWARD THE COURSE

THE JOURNEY to Jerez de la Frontera did not take long. Even if it had, John would not have cared. From the first, his experiences in Seville had sickened him. There was so little kindness in cities! People were too busy making money to care about courtesy or the finer things in life. It was easier to think of Heaven out in the country, where God's peace flowed like an endless benediction on the soul.

The Dominican priests in Jerez soon became John's loyal friends. Most of them agreed that the youth from Rivera would make a good friar—or at least a lay Brother.

"Why doesn't he see things this way?" an old priest asked the Father Prior one day. "He's been living here for nearly six months, talking about his trip to America, yet doing nothing about it."

"He could just as well receive the habit and consecrate himself to God," put in another. "What's the matter with him?"

The Prior shook his head. "I don't know. He has

a queer notion that God wants him to live in the world a while."

"How old is he, Father Prior?"

"Twenty-one."

"Well, he shouldn't wait too long or he might lose his vocation."

The Prior nodded. "I've told him that many times but he just smiles. Then he starts to talk about the heathen Indians in Peru, their poverty and ignorance. Really, our young friend is a strange soul. But a saint, of course. A real saint."

Most of the townsfolk in Jerez shared the Prior's opinion. Some even made it a habit to attend Mass at ten o'clock each morning in the Dominican church because John Masias was usually present and sometimes real wonders took place. For instance, it was quite evident that God often gave John a glimpse of Heaven. As he knelt, quiet and devout in his usual corner, his face would shine like the sun and those who had entered the church with heavy hearts would find themselves strangely encouraged. It was as though the young shepherd, seeing the beauties of Heaven, reflected them in his own person so that all about could take comfort in the fine reward God has in store for those who serve Him faithfully.

"He *is* a saint," said the townsfolk, echoing the sentiments of the Prior. "God always hears the prayers of that good young man."

Such talk, when it reached his ears, always made John feel uncomfortable. Gradually he began to visit the Dominican church less and less, fearful of the visions that occurred there and the resulting gossip. But his friendship for the friars did not cease. On the contrary, the young man found himself becoming quite attached to the Dominican Order.

As was only natural, he came to know quite a bit about the holy founder, too. He learned that Saint Dominic had established his religious family in the thirteenth century for the express purpose of preaching and teaching against the heresy of those days. Even now his friars were still warriors in the cause of truth, and though John had little schooling and therefore no preparation to be a friar, the thought did occur that it would be a wonderful thing to serve God as a Dominican lay Brother. He could do humble jobs about the monastery. He could see that the friars had good meals, that their habits were neat and clean and their rooms kept in order. He could be a warrior in white, too—in the white woolen habit of Saint Dominic's family.

"*Not yet*," said a little voice in his heart. "*Wait a while, John, before you think of entering religion.*"

Poor John! He knew how people talked of him at Jerez, how they came in crowds to the Dominican church and waited for God to grant him visions. He knew, too, that many believed he worked miracles, and that by now there were several colorful tales concerning his friendship with Saint John the Evangelist. Some even insisted that the holy Apostle was visible to him at all times, and his Guardian Angel as well. But no one ever thought of telling about the heartaches that went with the heavenly gifts. They never dreamed how hard it was to be given a glimpse of Heaven, to converse with a saint, then to be set adrift in the world again. Why, it was enough to make a person die of loneliness!

As the years passed, John was obedient to the inner voice that told him to remain at Jerez—in the world but not of it. He secured odd jobs about the town and patiently waited for God's Will to be made manifest. But sometimes he grew a little uneasy, particularly after he had passed his thirty-fourth birthday. Would he ever go to America at all? Would he ever wear the Dominican habit in some monastery in the New World and be a warrior in the cause of Christ?

"I've spent fourteen years here at Jerez," he told himself one day, a trifle sadly. "I'd willingly be a lay Brother at the Dominican convent but I still feel that isn't what God wants. Oh, dear Saint John! How much longer must I wait?"

As it turned out, this little prayer was answered rather quickly. No less a person than the Father Prior of the Dominican convent appeared at John's lodgings that same day with a remarkable piece of news. Recently a wealthy man had come to him with a problem. The man was a merchant, with large holdings in the New World. He was on his way now to San Lucar where a ship was waiting to take him across the Atlantic.

"I need a young man to travel with me," the merchant had explained anxiously. "Someone who will act as my personal servant and still keep my accounts. Do you know of anyone reliable, Father?"

"I recommended you, John," said the Father
Prior, watching the young man's face quietly. "I
guess the job is yours if you want it."

"Oh, Father! Of course I want it."

"Don't forget that it will be a dangerous trip, my
son. You may be shipwrecked. Or you may catch
some dreadful disease in the jungles."

John shook his head vigorously. Nothing mat-
tered save that at last there was a chance to secure
free passage to the New World. Yet even as he
rejoiced in the thought, he felt sudden pain. What
way was this to repay the kindness shown him by
the Dominicans in Jerez? For fourteen years they
had been his spiritual guides. They had secured for
him countless little jobs so that he could support
himself and his young sister back in Rivera. Now
it seemed that he was only too anxious to leave
them.

"Father, I'm only going because I think it's God's
Will," he added quickly. "And I don't expect things
to be easy. After all, there have been many martyrs
in America. So, will you please pray for me now
and then?"

The Prior nodded. His heart was heavy at losing
this beloved friend, yet the young man's sincere
conviction that he was doing the right thing was
comforting. By now the priest realized that John
was blessed by God in no ordinary way. It was quite
possible that he was divinely enlightened and spoke
the truth when he said that there was some great
work awaiting him in the New World.

"I'll remember you every day in Holy Mass," he

said reassuringly. "Don't worry about that. And now—would you like to meet the man for whom you're going to work?"

John nodded eagerly. "Oh, yes, Father! If it's not too much trouble for you."

The priest laughed. "Come along. He's waiting for us at the church. I told him we'd be there before Vespers."

So presently John was being introduced to the wealthy merchant, who took one look at his honest face and immediately accepted him as a traveling companion.

"You won't have many duties," he said kindly. "The main thing is that you keep an accurate record of my business affairs."

"Yes, sir," said John. "I understand."

A few days later, the young man and his master were on their way to the seacoast town of San Lucar. This trip did not take long, and presently John's eager heart realized its great ambition. He was on a boat at last! And the boat was en route to the New World—to Cartagena—that very important harbor in the south Caribbean!

"Thanks be to God!" he rejoiced. "Dear Apostle, please watch out for your little brother!"

The forty-day sea voyage was an uneventful one. There were no storms, no meetings with pirates, nothing but a succession of calm nights and sunny days. John was never weary of gazing at the many new sights, and whenever the ship passed close to an island, he stood by the railing and peered long and earnestly at the copper-colored natives in the

distance, the luxuriant trees and plants, which told
that the vessel was now in tropical waters. At such
times his heart beat fast as he thought of the great
good an honest Christian could do in these wild
jungles. What joy to teach the Holy Faith to these
ignorant souls! To bring the saving waters of Baptism to little children! Yet it was still Peru that
claimed his chief interest. After all, he felt that it
was among the pagans in this great land of gold and
silver that he would spend his days. Other men
might travel to this fabulous country to make fortunes for themselves. He, by the grace of God, had
been given a far greater work to do.

It came as a real shock when the merchant called
him one morning, just as the ship was entering the
harbor of Cartagena, and announced that his
employment was at an end.

"You're not too good at figures, John. I just have
to get another helper with more schooling than you
to keep my accounts."

At once anxiety filled the young man's heart.
"You don't mean there's any money missing, sir?"

"Your writing is so bad that I can't tell. Listen,
young friend—how many years did you spend in
getting an education?"

Deep color flooded John's cheeks. "I never went
to school, sir. I...I...just picked up a little writing and arithmetic by myself."

"*You never went to school?*"

"No, sir. You see, I was left an orphan before I
was five years old. At first my uncle looked after
my little sister and me, but he didn't have too much

money and so finally he put me out to work. I was a shepherd until I was twenty. After that, I went to Seville and then to Jerez. When I met you, I was. . .well, a handyman of sorts at the Dominican convent."

The merchant shifted uneasily. "John, I had no idea things were so difficult for you. Now it's much harder to say I can't keep you with me. But business is business, you know. . ."

John nodded. "It's quite all right, sir. I understand. And please don't worry about me. I'll find some other job."

"I hope so, young friend. You see, I like you. And it hurts to cast you adrift like this in a strange country."

The young man smiled. Being left to his own resources was no new thing. It had happened so many times in Spain.

"Don't worry, sir," he said cheerfully. "I'll manage to get along somehow. And I'll say a prayer that I didn't make too many mistakes in figuring out your accounts."

The two parted then, with a hearty handshake, and John turned to the business of proceeding with his journey. Cartagena was the last important harbor before the Isthmus of Panama. Even if he had kept his job, it would have been necessary to say good-bye to the ship. From now on, in order to reach the west coast of South America, it would be necessary to walk or ride through hundreds of miles of dense jungle. Or one could go by native canoe up one of the many hidden waterways that

led to the interior. Later, one could scale the mountains of Colombia and Ecuador and proceed to
Peru down the barren wastelands of the Pacific
coast.

"Dear Saint John!" he said softly. "I need your
help. Will you come again, please, and show me
what to do?"

Even as he spoke these words, the young man's
heart gave a great leap of joy. A strange mist was
obscuring the busy seaport of Cartagena! Gone
were the great ships riding at anchor, the mixture
of black men, yellow men, white men, who
crowded the docks. Once more his hand felt the
grasp of his heavenly friend's and his ears heard the
beloved voice bidding him not to be afraid.

"Look up, little brother," it whispered. "See my
country. This is where live the blessed souls who
did God's Will while they lived on earth. Is it not
worth the few lonely years that men must spend
in the world?"

John looked up, and his heart swelled with joy.
Heaven! Once again God's Mercy was granting him
that vision. And how beautiful it was! There were
no words to describe the Majesty of God, the peace
and glory of His saints!

HEAVEN! ONCE AGAIN GOD'S MERCY WAS
GRANTING HIM THAT VISION.

CHAPTER 5

THE CITY OF THE KINGS

HOW LONG the vision lasted, John could, as usual, not say. All he knew was that finally the strange mist vanished, and he found himself in Cartagena once more, alone and friendless. Yet deep in his heart he knew what God wished him to do. He was not to make his way westward after all. He was to go to the east, to the port of Barranquilla on the Magdalena river. Here he would receive help and further instructions.

Accordingly, the young man turned his back on the ship that had brought him to the New World and resolutely set out for Barranquilla. To his dismay, the country soon became wild and the heat oppressive. As he pushed his way through the dense tropical growth, he was almost tempted to despair. There were so many fierce animals in these jungles! And poisonous snakes! How could he ever make his way unharmed through the green wilderness? And what would he do about food?

"Saint John, you'll have to help me," he said simply. "There's no other way I can keep alive. And

I'm worried. Why is it I am told to go east instead of west? This is not the way to reach Peru."

Yes—God was testing John's faith once more. But in a short time he realized why, for in Barranquilla he met a group of cheerful adventurers who were about to sail up the Magdalena river for the interior of the continent. This, it seems, was by far the best way to reach the south. There was less danger from prowling beasts.

"Why don't you come with us?" they asked John. "We could use a young man like you."

"But I haven't any money, good sirs!"

The travelers laughed. "You'll earn your passage as you go. See that big canoe? It belongs to us. You can help paddle it. Now what do you say?"

The offer was an acceptable one and in a few minutes John found himself a member of the little party. From the beginning one thing was clear: his companions were making this trip for one reason only. They wanted to find the gold that was known to lie hidden in the Andes. They seemed particularly interested in reaching Bogota, a mountain city where men had been known to become wealthy overnight. John's indifference to such good fortune puzzled them at first, but they did not argue about it. After all, their own chances for becoming rich were slightly increased thereby. Besides, why argue with a fellow traveler? In such wild country it was well for Spaniards to remain together as friends. There was no telling when hostile natives, hiding in the dense trees, would spring upon them. If this happened, a united group would have a better chance at survival than a lone individual.

As the days passed and the big canoe moved safely from one river port to the next, John's companions marveled still more at his unusual ways. Never before had they known a man to say the Rosary three times a day; to act toward God as a child acts toward its father, expecting Him to be always interested in human joys and sorrows. Could it be possible that John Masias really was a grown man of thirty-four years?

Eventually, they became convinced that this wayfarer was an extraordinary person. "The strange thing is, his prayers do seem to bring results," whispered one of them, with an air of discovery. "Why, we haven't had any trouble with the Indians during the whole trip."

"And we've never lacked food," put in another. "Or come down with the fever. I say it's a good thing we brought John along."

"Maybe he'll change his mind and stay with us in Bogota," said a third traveler. "We could probably find a lot of gold if he prayed for us."

John, however, was still anxious to reach Peru as soon as possible. When the group finally arrived in Bogota, the city that stood more than eight thousand feet above the sea, he bade his friends a courteous farewell. Yes—he would pray for their success, but he could stay with them no longer.

"But you can't go to Peru alone!" they cried. "It would be suicide even to try!"

John smiled. Then he tried to explain that God would look after him. If it was His Will that one

HE BEGAN TO CROSS
THE NORTHERN ANDES ON FOOT.

young Spaniard should meet death in the mountains, what did it matter? Heaven was worth this
or any other suffering.

True to his prophecy, John was wonderfully pro-
tected during the next few weeks. A stranger, and
with no one to advise or console him, he began the
hazardous task of crossing the northern Andes on
foot. One day he would be scaling snow-clad peaks.
The next, making his way across the extensive val-
leys that few white men ever had seen. Indians
lived in these parts, but they did no harm to the
traveler. John even made friends with a few of them
and tried to tell them of God. This was not easy,
since he was ignorant of their language. Yet they
learned to make the Sign of the Cross and in gratitude gave him food, pointed out the poisonous
plants and berries that were not safe to touch, and
finally provided him with a mule for his journey.

"Quito," they told him one day, smiling as he
gazed in puzzled fashion at the surrounding country. As they spoke they pointed to the southwest.

John understood. Quito was the great city built
on the Equator. Nearly ten thousand feet above the
sea, it was one more milestone on the long journey
to Peru. With God's help he would go there, rest
a while, then proceed as his heart directed.

A month later, as he rode his mule down a wind-
ing mountain path, John's eyes beheld a happy
sight. Before him were miles and miles of glistening
water. It was the Pacific Ocean at last! The barren
stretches of sand and rock told him his course had
been right.

"Thank God!" he cried, and dismounted from his mule to kneel in thanksgiving. A half hour later he looked up to see an Indian boy peering at him cautiously. The lad seemed about ten years old and was dressed in rags.

John smiled as he arose from his knees. "Good morning, little brother. And what is your name?"

The boy scowled. For a moment it seemed as though he might run away, fearful of the stranger who had been kneeling in the middle of the path. Seeing this, John stretched out his hand.

"Don't be afraid. I won't hurt you."

Minutes passed and the boy's dark eyes continued to rest suspiciously upon the newcomer. The thought flashed through John's mind that possibly the lad knew no other language than his Indian tongue. It was a surprise therefore when the latter suddenly burst into speech.

"I'm Michael! I'm hungry!"

John smiled. "So you're hungry, are you? Well, little friend, I have some food in my pack. Dried figs and raisins. Does that suit you?"

The boy nodded and stretched out a bony hand. For the moment hunger was triumphing over fear!

As time passed, Michael's strangeness melted away, and he began to confide his brief life's history to John. It seemed he was an orphan. His mother had died when he was born; his father, from hardship as a slave in the silver mines. He himself kept alive by begging in the streets of Lima.

"_Lima!_" cried John. "Then the city isn't far from here?"

The boy nodded. "About ten miles. If you keep
to this path you won't miss it. Or. . ." and he hesitated shyly, "I could show you the way."

John smiled. It was quite evident that the youngster did not want to leave him. His fears were completely gone now, and he seemed eager to prove
his gratitude for the food given to him. "All right,"
he said. "You ride the mule, Michael, and tell me
some more about yourself. The time ought to pass
more pleasantly then."

The boy's account of conditions in Lima touched
John's heart. The newly-arrived Spaniards were in
complete control of the city. Most of them were
very rich. As for the Indians who once had owned
Peru, they were treated as slaves. Their lands had
been taken away by the white people. They were
forced to work in the mines, where most of them
died of hardship.

"Like my father," said Michael. "Oh, John! How
we Indians hate the rich white people!"

For a moment John was silent. How could he tell
his little friend that hatred of any sort was wrong?

"Not all Spaniards are unkind," he said finally.
"Surely there are some priests in Lima who help
the poor?"

Michael nodded. "Oh, yes. The Spanish priests
tell us about the real God. They tell us someday
we Indians will be happy in Heaven because of our
sufferings. These Spaniards we like, because they
teach and help us. But the others, no! We would
kill them if we could."

Late in the afternoon, John and his young guide

entered Lima. The city had been founded on the Feast of the Epiphany in 1535, and for this reason it was called "The City of the Kings," commemorating the three Wise Men who had brought gifts to the Infant Christ. The young Spaniard sighed, recalling that the title was hardly a fitting one. The Wise Men had given generously to a poor little Family in Bethlehem, but few of his wealthy countrymen had given anything to the natives of Peru. They had taken instead—gold and silver, the freedom of a peace-loving people.

"May their sins be blotted out by future saints!" John prayed, "by other Spaniards who have brought one gift at least—the gift of the true Faith!"

Because he had asked him to do so, Michael presently led John to the nearest church—that of San Lazaro. This was a poor little building at the extreme edge of the city. After a brief thanksgiving for his safe arrival, the young man came outside to survey the neighborhood. Regretfully, he realized that Michael had been right. Poverty was everywhere in this section of Lima. Some of the Indians and Negroes crowding the narrow street were living skeletons, dirty and diseased. As for the children, what a dreadful sight these poor little ones presented!

"Can't we go now?" begged Michael, pulling at John's sleeve. "This isn't a nice place to stay."

John shook his head. "I'd like to speak to a few of these good souls first."

"No, no! Don't do that!"

"Why not?"

"Because some are lepers. I wouldn't have brought you here, but you said I had to take you to the nearest church. Oh, John! Please don't stay! Please don't!"

Reluctantly, the young man let himself be led away. The mule followed obediently, and in a few minutes they had left behind the evil-smelling atmosphere of San Lazaro. Almost immediately the Rimac river came into view and the stone bridge which connected the poor section of Lima with the newer part. Many people were crowding the bridge, for there was a large market nearby where meat, fruit and vegetables were on sale.

"I think I can get you a job," said Michael as they made their way toward one of the stands. "See that big man smiling at us? Over there by the meat?"

John nodded. "Who is it, Michael?"

"A friend of mine. Peter Jimines Menacho. He owns a big cattle ranch outside the city. Twice a week he comes here with fresh meat to sell. He's been very good to me, and I think maybe he'll help you, too."

Slowly the man and boy pushed their way through the bustling crowd. John looked about in bewilderment, for there was a great babble of strange tongues on every side. Silver coins were changing hands with amazing speed as men and women bargained eagerly. Everywhere was the smell of fruit, of strange food being cooked over open fires. The scene was colorful, yet not without its tragic touch. Scores of beggars were crouching in the gutter, their pitiful voices raised in quest of alms. John's heart ached. Very few of the shoppers seemed to be noticing God's poor.

Finding that his friend was ready to stop to give the beggars a word of encouragement, Michael grabbed his arm briskly. "Don't pay any attention to them," he said. "There are too many for you to help. Besides, we mustn't lose any time if you're to get a job before nightfall."

John laughed at the businesslike attitude of his young friend. "A job before nightfall? But there's no rush, Michael. I don't need to find work right away."

The boy stared. "Aren't you poor? Don't you need a place to sleep tonight?"

"Yes. And I will have to find work in a little while. That's why I thought I might go to see the Dominican priests first. They may have some work for me in their monastery."

Michael shook his head. "Come along," he said. "You can make much more money on my friend's ranch."

CHAPTER 6

A SON OF SAINT DOMINIC

JOHN WORKED for Peter Menacho during the next two and one-half years. His duties were similar to those he had known as a farm helper in Spain, since they consisted mainly in caring for the sheep and cattle on the Menacho ranch. The young Spaniard seemed happy in such work, yet at Christmas time in the year 1621 he came to his employer with a startling piece of news. He had finally made up his mind as to how he wished to spend the rest of his life. In a month or so he would be giving up his present employment for a new work.

The rancher was beside himself. "You can't leave me now!" he cried. "You're the best worker I've ever had. Just tell me how much extra money you want and I'll gladly pay it."

"It isn't a question of money, sir. You've always been more than generous."

"But you must have found a better job. Where is it, John? Who has stolen you from me?"

The young man smiled. "I am going away to be

a religious," he said softly. "God willing, I shall ask for the Dominican habit next month."

Peter Menacho stared. "*You're going to be a priest?*"

"No, sir. Only a lay Brother. Will you pray that I be a good one?"

The older man's disappointment was intense. John Masias would be impossible to replace. Who else had such skill in handling animals, in curing their illnesses?

"You're too old to be going into religion," he said bluntly. "That life is for the young, John. Take my advice. Stay here on the ranch. Say as many prayers as you like. Only don't leave me for the cloister."

Although John admired his employer very much, such words could not change his mind. Now that he was thirty-seven years old, he felt sure that God's plans for him were clear. Peru needed saints, souls who would atone for the greed of their Spanish brothers by prayer and sacrifice. Well, he would try to be one of these souls. He would become a Dominican lay Brother and make his life one long act of reparation for the sins of his fellow countrymen.

There were two Dominican monasteries in Lima: that of the Most Holy Rosary (popularly called Santo Domingo) and a smaller house dedicated to Saint Mary Magdalen. The latter was known as the Magdalena, and everyone knew that real saints lived within its walls. After all, the Dominicans of the Magdalena did not engage in active works, such as teaching and preaching. They spent most of their

time in prayer, meditation and works of penance.
In such a way they called down God's blessing on
other members of the Order who could not follow
such a rigorous regime.

After due thought, John decided that it was to
this smaller group of the Dominican family that
God was calling him. The decision made his heart
leap for joy, but Peter Menacho was far from shar-
ing in such enthusiasm.

"Life at the Magdalena is terribly hard," he said.
"Are you sure you're not making a mistake by going
there?"

John smiled. "A mistake? Oh, no, sir! God has
given me very good health. I'll be able to manage.
And I'd like to ask you one favor."

"What's that?"

"I expect to stay with you for another month.
Could I have my wages in advance, please? And
divided into three parts?"

"Of course, John. But why?"

"I have a sister living in Spain, sir. Her name is
Mary. I'd like to send her part of my savings. There's
a boat leaving next week and if it's not asking too
much . . ."

Peter Menacho nodded. "That's all right, John.
You give me your sister's address and I'll see that
the money goes to her. As for the rest of your earn-
ings, have you some other plans?"

"I'd like one-third to be given to the poor, sir,
and the balance to Brother Paul at the Magdalena.
That good soul will be able to put everything to
proper use."

It was a few weeks later, on the afternoon of January 22, 1622, when John Masias said good-bye to his friends on the ranch and made his way into the city of Lima. His heart was beating wildly. He had been on many travels, had experienced many exciting adventures, but this surely was the greatest of all. That same night, as the friars of the Magdalena were assembled for Matins, he would die to the world! He would give himself to the service of God for the rest of his life!

As the white adobe towers of the monastery finally came into view, he breathed a short and familiar prayer. "Saint John, be with me! Help me to be a saint!"

Brother Paul of Charity, the keeper of the monastery gate, was waiting for the newcomer as he rang the bell. Known throughout the city as a saint himself, one who was the loyal friend of every sick and needy person, he had been acquainted with John Masias for a long time, had prayed for him and encouraged him to be a Dominican. Now his face was wreathed with smiles. At midnight, just as the feast of the great Saint Raymond of Pennafort began, his young friend would be clothed in the black and white habit of Saint Dominic's family!

"Everything's ready for tonight," he announced cheerfully. "Come inside and let me have a look at you."

Promptly John entered the little wooden house, close to the gate, where Brother Paul spent so many hours attending to the needs of the poor. As he did so the latter stared in amazement, for John was not wearing his usual clothes. His feet were bare and about his shoulders was the rough woolen blanket of an Indian beggar.

"John! What's the meaning of this?"

The young man smiled. "Do I look different, Brother? Well, there's a reason. Just before leaving the ranch I exchanged clothes with a poor man. It seemed. . .well, a good way to say farewell to my old life."

There was affectionate understanding in Brother Paul's glance. Ten years ago he had come to the Magdalena in just the same spirit of abandonment. He had had nothing to offer God but love and eagerness to serve Him. Yet his little gift had been accepted. God had taken his human nothingness and made it great. He had given a poor lay Brother the wonderful task of leading other hearts to Himself through works of charity.

Brother Paul was not able to give full expression to such thoughts, however, for presently the Prior sent word that John Masias was to attend Vespers.

"You'd better go right away," said the older man. "Obedience is one of the first rules in the religious life, you know."

John nodded. "I'm ready, Brother. Shall I go alone?"

Brother Paul opened the door of his little house. "No. I'll take you. And listen, my son. It's almost five o'clock. You still have seven hours to think about the step you are going to take. If you want to change your mind. . ."

"Brother Paul!"

The words were uttered with such earnestness that the older man laughed in spite of himself. "All right," he said. "I won't argue with you. After all, I've always felt you belonged with us. May God bless you, John, as He has blessed me these past ten years!"

Late that night, a few minutes before midnight, the friars of the Magdalena arose from their hard beds and made their way to the chapel for Matins. Because it was an important feast day in the Order, that of Saint Raymond of Pennafort, four altar candles had been lighted by the sacristan instead of the usual two. By the light of these the priests and Brothers found their places in the choir stalls while the Prior, Father Salvador Ramirez, seated himself in a chair before the altar. For a moment all was quiet as the community knelt in prayer. Then the Prior gave a signal and John came slowly forward. His face was glowing with happiness, and the older priests and Brothers smiled at the sight. Well they knew what was taking place in the newcomer's heart. It was always the same when a poor human creature gave himself to God.

The Prior had similar thoughts as he saw the young man advance toward him and kneel at his feet. "What do you ask?" he inquired kindly.

"God's mercy and yours," replied John.

At this another friar stepped forward. In his hands he bore the white woolen tunic, hood, leather belt and black scapular of the Dominican Order. The poor raiment of a beggar which John had been wearing was removed, and presently the new Brother lay prostrate before his superior. This humble action caused him great joy, for it proved his nothingness before the assembled community.

As the Prior gave a slight knock on the arm of his chair, he arose obediently, then knelt to hear the words of welcome addressed to him. A few minutes later, while the familiar strains of the *Veni Creator* filled the air, he left his place to greet each of his new brethren with the kiss of peace. How happy he was! Never again would he have to worry about the future, about where to live or what to do with his time. He was a religious at last, and for him the will of his superiors would always be the Will of God.

Such joy remained with him throughout the chanting of Matins and Lauds. He was still pondering his good fortune when the signal came for the community to retire from the chapel for a few hours' rest. Obediently John arose from his knees and followed his companions into the darkened corridor. He knew where to go without asking questions, for a cell had been assigned to him shortly after his arrival. He needed only to walk to the end of the corridor and climb one flight of stairs. His little room was then only a few steps away.

John was halfway up the flight of stairs when a frightening thing happened. A rough hand gripped him by the shoulder. Try though he would, he could not move an inch.

"What is it?" he whispered, knowing that it was the time of the "Great Silence" when no friar spoke except in case of grave necessity.

VENI CREATOR SPIRITUS ✠

HOW HAPPY HE WAS! HE WAS A RELIGIOUS AT LAST!

There was no answer. Fearfully John peered into the darkness to see who was holding him back. As he did so, a hateful voice hissed in his ear.

"So you think you're going to be happy here, do you? Well, wait and see, Brother John. Wait and see."

The next thing he knew, he felt a violent push. He reached out a hand to save himself, but it was too late. He was falling headlong down the stairs!

Poor John! Bruised and shaken, he finally picked himself up. There was no doubt about it. The voice he had heard, the rough hand on his shoulder, had been that of the Devil who was trying to frighten him on his first night at the Magdalena so that he might give up his religious vocation.

Trembling, the young man reached for the large wooden rosary which hung from his belt. "Jesus, Mary, Joseph!" he whispered. "Look after me!"

These words had a sudden and wonderful effect. Deep in his heart John knew that the devil had fled, for he could not bear that anyone speak the Holy Names in his presence. Nor could he remain where holy water was being used. Comforted with such knowledge, John climbed the stairs again, this time without mishap. As soon as he reached his cell, he dipped his fingers into the holy water font near the door and made the Sign of the Cross, slowly and reverently. Then, as the Rule of the monastery demanded, he removed his shoes and lay down upon his bed fully clothed.

"I mustn't expect to find the religious life easy," he told himself. "I know the Devil is angry because I have promised to be a saint. But what of it? The next time he tries to hurt me, I'll ask God's help as I did just now. There won't be any need to be afraid of him then."

CHAPTER 7

KEEPER OF THE GATE

JOHN HAD MANY an occasion to practice patience in the next few weeks, for the Devil plagued him almost constantly. Before long, the friars grew accustomed to seeing the new lay Brother with a bruised eye or a cut lip. No words were needed to explain that the powers of Hell had attacked him the night before.

"Usually the Devil works in a sly fashion," they thought. "He doesn't show himself to people but uses trials and troubles to weaken their faith in God. But with Brother John things are much different. The Devil knows he can't break his spirit, so he tries to hurt his body."

Because of John's nightly encounters with Satan, the Prior readily gave permission for extra holy water fonts to be placed throughout the convent, also for blessed candles to be lighted on the stairs. Brother John was to have all possible help in his battles with Hell. This was a little embarrassing to the newcomer, who had never wanted to attract attention.

"Don't worry too much," said Brother Paul one morning, noticing fresh bruises on his young friend's face. "Brother Martin de Porres also has trouble with the Devil, and he's a real saint."

"I've heard of Brother Martin. Doesn't he live at our other convent?"

The older Brother nodded. "That's right. He's been at Santo Domingo since he was fifteen. That should be. . .well, about twenty-eight years. And let me tell you this: Peru never had a greater son than Martin de Porres. You must get to know him."

But the months passed and John had no opportunity of meeting Brother Martin. His days were very full, for the Prior had placed him in one of the busiest spots in the monastery: the little house by the gate where Brother Paul of Charity attended to the needs of the poor. Every morning he came here to prepare the food and clothing that would be given away after the friars' noon meal.

He loved this work. More than that, he loved Brother Paul, who he felt was a real saint, and his heart rejoiced that the Prior had made him the good man's assistant. Yet, from the beginning, Brother Paul insisted that John should know the truth about him. His life had not always been that of a good Christian. In Spain, where he had been known as Ferdinand Palomeque, he had spent many years in sin. Only God's mercy had saved him from Hell.

"When I came to the New World, the Lord gave me the grace to be a religious," he said one day, tears glistening in his eyes. "Dear Brother, how little I have deserved such kindness!"

John found it hard to believe that his good friend had been a sinner, yet other members of the community assured him it was so. Eleven years ago, on his entrance into the Magdalena, it had been necessary for Brother Paul to undergo many trials before the superiors were convinced he had a real vocation. His testing period in the novitiate had been doubled, and he had been moved from one work to another before being given the important task of gatekeeper. Now, however, all agreed that Brother Paul's conversion was genuine, and many tales were told concerning the power of his prayers. There were even some who had felt a strange heat coming from his heart. It was an overflow, they said, of the love for God and souls which burned within him.

As a novice, John set himself to imitate Brother Paul, to learn all he could from this saintly friend. His work as a lay Brother in the Dominican Order rapidly became uppermost in his mind and he thought a great deal about the meaning of his new role.

"I have come here to be useful to the priests," he decided. "They have no time to prepare meals, to sweep and cook and mend. These things are for the lay Brothers. Dear Lord, help me to do my work well!"

God was pleased with such sincerity. One day the Prior called John to his cell and told him that in a week's time he was to make his profession, his solemn promise to remain with the Dominican

Order until death.

"You have done remarkably well as a novice," said the superior, "and this matter of your profession is by way of a reward. Are you surprised, Brother?"

Surprised? John could hardly speak! Well he knew that a lay Brother at the Magdalena never made his profession after only one year's trial in the novitiate. Generally three years had to pass before such an important step could be taken.

"I don't deserve this honor," he faltered. "Brother Paul had to make his novitiate twice... and he's a real saint..."

The Prior was not interested in such objections. "You will make your profession a year and two days from the time you entered," he said. "That will be next week, on January 25, 1623. How old will you be then?"

"Almost thirty-eight, Father."

There was real confusion in the young man's voice, and the Prior smiled in spite of himself. "Let's say I'm allowing you to make an early profession because you're not an ignorant boy," he suggested. "Does that make you feel better?"

The excuse did not deceive John, but he made no more objections. After all, the word of the Prior was law. It was not the place of a lay Brother to argue what was or was not best.

"Yes, Father," he said. "Thank you very much."

He would have withdrawn then, but the superior held up his hand. "Wait a minute, Brother John. I want to ask you some questions. First of all, who has taught you most about the religious life since you came here?"

John smiled with relief. There was no danger now that the Prior would compliment him further on his virtue. "Brother Paul of Charity," he answered quickly. "He has taught me nearly everything I know."

"For instance?"

"Well, how to be unselfish."

"*Unselfish?* But surely you had learned this before you came to the Magdalena?"

"Not exactly, Father Prior."

"What do you mean by that? Come now, speak up and don't be shy."

John's fingers found the rosary at his side and clutched the beads fervently. The old confusion was upon him once more, for the conversation was turning away from Brother Paul to the spiritual secrets of John's own life. Yet the Prior had spoken and he must be obeyed.

"I mean...oh, Father Prior, it's hard to put it into words, but when I first came here Brother Paul told me that the Catholic Church is one big family."

"Yes. Go on, Brother."

"If a Christian is good, if he says just a simple prayer, he helps all other Christians to grow in grace—plus, he brings poor pagan souls closer to the Church. And if a Christian is bad, if he laughs at God's Commandments and spends his time foolishly, he hurts all other men. Perhaps I did know this before I came here, in a dim and hidden way, but it was Brother Paul who made everything clear."

For a moment the older religious was silent.

Although a lay Brother's vocation was not to write books or to preach sermons, the words John had just spoken were worthy of a great scholar or preacher. In them was the secret of true peace. But just now the Prior was not ready to show further admiration of his young friend.

"Very interesting," he said casually. "Then you really believe that if a person says one Hail Mary devoutly, he's helping the rest of us to go to Heaven?"

"Yes, Father Prior. I believe it with all my heart."

"And if he tells a lie, or steals, he is hurting not only himself but the whole world?"

"That's right, Father. To me, all Catholics on earth are like the links in a great chain, with Christ as the lock that holds them together. The lock will never give way but the links can grow rusty and break. Or they can be kept well oiled and strong by prayer, and new links can be added. Brother Paul taught me this the first day I was his helper."

The Prior cast a shrewd glance at the young man before him. "You seem to rely a great deal on Brother Paul. What would you do if he were taken away?"

In spite of himself John's eyes grew wide with alarm. "I should miss him as I have never missed any other friend, Father Prior."

"And you would let it affect your work?"

"Oh, no! With God's help, I would still try to do my duty. But it would be very hard sometimes. I know it."

"Good," said the Prior. "I'm glad you realize that

friends are given to us for one reason only: to help us save our souls, to lead us to God, not to rest content with them. Well, you may go back to your duties now, Brother. I'm glad we've had this little talk."

"Yes, Father Prior," said John. "And thank you again for letting me be professed so soon."

The next few days were busy ones. John thought and prayed about the great grace of religious profession that soon would be his. In a little while he would make a solemn promise to be obedient to his superiors in all things. Because of this promise, everything he did for the rest of his life would have more merit in God's sight, would strengthen and increase the invisible chain formed by Catholic souls.

"Dear Lord, help me to be always faithful to my promise!" he prayed. "Don't let my own little link become rusty and broken. Let me be strong with Your strength. Let me help others to be strong, too."

There was need for John to offer such prayers, for within a year following his profession a bad sore formed on one knee and he was sent away to the mountains to recover from the infection. When he returned two months later, he found that Brother Paul was no longer at the Magdalena. The good soul had been transferred to Santo Domingo—the larger and older Dominican convent in Lima.

"Dear God!" thought John fearfully, remembering his former conversation with the Prior. "Who will have charge of the poor now?"

JOHN HAD FULL CHARGE OF THE NEEDY FOLK
WHO CAME EACH DAY TO THE MONASTERY.

This question was soon answered. Within a few
minutes of his arrival, John was informed that he
himself had been appointed gatekeeper. From now
on he would have full charge of the more than two
hundred needy folk who came each day to the
monastery.

Poor John! He was almost beside himself with
anxiety. His best friend had been taken away! More
than that. He, a religious of only two years' standing, was expected to fill his place! Slowly he made
his way to the gatekeeper's lodge, closed the door
behind him, then knelt before the large crucifix his
old friend had loved so much.

"What am I going to do?" he cried, stretching
forth his arms to Heaven. "Saint John the Evangelist, will you tell me?"

Time passed. The canaries that had been Brother
Paul's special pets chirped and sang cheerfully from
their cages by the window. The friars entered the
church to chant the Office, then returned to their
various works. Still John prayed, earnestly and
devoutly, as a child who relies completely on his
father's goodness.

"Dear God, You have given me this new work
to do," he whispered. "Will You leave me alone
without the means to do it?"

Suddenly a thought flashed through the lay
Brother's mind. Why not ask certain wealthy people to aid him with donations of food, clothes and
money? Brother Paul had done this from time to
time, and always with success. Surely Doctor
Balthazar Carrasco would help. Then there were

Peter Ramirez and his sister Beatrice. And Anthony de Alarcon and Peter de Garate.

"I'll write little notes to each," thought John eagerly. "I'll explain how worried I am at having to look after so many poor people."

With a sigh of relief he arose from his knees. The writing of five letters would not be easy, for a lack of education still prevented much skill with pen or pencil. However, John was not worried now. Once again God had been merciful. He had allowed the holy Apostle to answer his prayers for help.

He was only halfway through his second letter when the bell at the gate began to ring, a sign that some poor person was waiting to speak with him. Quickly he arose and went to the small window in the door. A shabbily dressed woman was standing there and weeping bitterly. At once the need for letterwriting vanished from John's mind.

"What's the trouble?" he asked quickly. "Are you sick?"

The woman shook her head, then sank to the ground in a pathetic heap. "No, Brother. I just want a coat. Any kind of coat will do. . .old or dirty. . .it doesn't matter. . ."

Gently he helped his visitor to her feet. "There, there," he said comfortingly. "I haven't a lady's coat today but I'll get one for you, never fear. I'll write to someone I know. . ."

At this the woman began to cry as though her heart would break. "No, Brother John, I've got to have a coat right away! My two daughters haven't anything to wear. . .they can't even go to Mass. . .

Oh, I'm so ashamed and unhappy!"

Bit by bit the unfortunate story was poured into John's ears. The woman was a widow, and penniless. As a last resource she had borrowed some clothes from a neighbor to make this trip to the Magdalena. Her daughters were quite sure she would come home with at least one coat for them.

John's heart ached at this tale of poverty and wretchedness. "I'll get a coat for you, but it will take time," he said slowly. "Perhaps if you come here tomorrow. . ."

The woman was desperate. "I won't leave this place until you've helped me!" she sobbed. "Dear Brother, give me a coat for my girls! In God's Name, don't turn me away!"

John sighed. "All right," he said. "Wait here. I'll see what I can do."

In just a few minutes he had gained the seclusion of his little cell. Quickly he went to a large chest by the window. Sometimes he put aside gifts for the poor in this place, bringing them later to the house by the gate.

"Dear Saint John, please let me find the right kind of coat!" he whispered. "I'm pretty sure there are only men's clothes here, but perhaps, while I was away. . ."

Suddenly his heart gave a great leap. A woman's coat, neatly folded, lay on top of the various pieces of wearing apparel! And it was new!

Grateful tears filled his eyes as he knelt down beside the chest. How foolish for him to have worried at being made the keeper of the gate!

CHAPTER 8

SAINTS FOR AMERICA

VERY SOON the community realized that John was a worthy successor to Brother Paul of Charity. The incident of the woman who had wanted a coat had been witnessed by Father Gonzalez de Guzman. This priest could not get over his amazement at the wonderful way in which God had answered the lay Brother's prayers.

"We have a real treasure in John Masias," he told the Prior. "Somehow I think the New World has found another saint in him."

The Prior nodded, then repeated the conversation he had had with John some time ago, the conversation which so aptly described the meaning of the Mystical Body of Christ.

"The good soul thinks we are all links in a chain," he said slowly. "He believes that Christ is the lock which holds this chain together. If one of us is weak, it makes the chain weak, too, in spite of the powerful lock. Then we have wars and persecutions. What do you think of such an idea, Father?"

The priest was silent a moment. "It's very well

71

put," he said finally. "But how did an unlettered lay Brother obtain such knowledge?"

The Prior smiled. "From Brother Paul, he says. Yet I believe John has had equally fine thoughts and only humility makes him keep them to himself. After all, real wisdom is the fruit of prayer and John is always praying. Haven't you noticed?"

Father Gonzalez agreed that the gatekeeper took very little rest from prayer. Generally he rang the bell at midnight to call the friars to chapel. The same was true at dawn, when it was again time to chant God's praises. In between, John was either with his poor, giving out food and clothes and sound advice, or in the chapel on his knees.

"I'm going to watch this lay Brother," said Father Gonzalez emphatically. "I think I can learn a great deal from him."

John never guessed that he was soon the object of real admiration on the part of Father Gonzalez de Guzman. For one thing, he was too busy. For another, his was the humility of the wise man who realizes he is alive and blessed with an immortal soul only through the mercy of God. As a result, he never made the mistake of feeling proud or self-sufficient because of the many unusual graces given him. Even as a child he had realized that to be granted visions of Heaven, of saints and angels, does not mean a person is a saint. Such things are free gifts of God, bestowed upon some and withheld from others. They are never necessary for salvation.

"Love is all that matters," John often thought.

"Love of God, then love of neighbor. Oh, I must never forget these two great commandments! They are the tools that will help any man to go to Heaven."

Although he had little free time, the gatekeeper learned quite a bit about the history of Peru—the country of his adoption. As a boy he had known that most people left Europe for the New World in order to seek their fortunes in the Andes. In this great chain of mountains, running the length of South America, were rich deposits of gold and silver. Hundreds had become wealthy overnight by claiming these hidden treasures for themselves.

However, John was more interested in two Spaniards who had never bothered looking for gold. These men had gained the only fortune that counts. They had saved their souls. They had done untold good for the ignorant natives. One of these was the second Archbishop of Lima, Turribius Alphonsus de Mogrovejo, who had died in 1606. The other was a Franciscan missionary, Father Francis Solano, who had gone to his reward in 1610. Then there was a native Peruvian girl, equaling both men in sanctity. She was Rose de Flores, a Dominican Tertiary. She had died in 1617.

"I wish I could have known these wonderful people," John told the Prior one day. "What a pity that I only arrived in Lima after the three of them were dead!"

The superior agreed, then gave the younger religious a searching glance. "Brother John, I want to ask you something."

"Yes, Father Prior?"

"Are you feeling well these days? Is your knee all right again?"

John was startled at the anxiety in the priest's voice. "Why, of course!" he said cheerfully. "You sent me to the mountains for two months, Father Prior, and I didn't come back until the sore was healed. I'm really feeling very well. And I love the work you've given me to do."

The Prior was relieved. "All right, Brother, I believe you. But it won't hurt to have a little vacation once in a while. How about the tenth day of each month?"

John was overcome at the kindly suggestion for he had not become a Dominican in order to enjoy a life of ease but that he might have many works of prayer and penance to offer God for the salvation of souls. However, there was no need to worry because the Prior wished him to have one day a month for his own needs. Obedience was the chief virtue in the religious life, of even greater importance than prayer and sacrifice.

"Thank you, Father," he said gratefully. "It will be very nice to have a day for myself now and then."

The first of John's little holidays fell upon a very important date—February 10, 1624. On this day the Monastery of Santa Catalina, first convent for Dominican nuns in Lima, was scheduled to be dedicated. The night before the important event, the gatekeeper made arrangements with two other Brothers to care for the poor who might come to the Magdalena while he was away. Then, very early in the morning, he set out for the new monastery. As he walked, Brother John's mind was busy with many thoughts. Chief among these was the question of sanctity in America. Through the centuries, John reflected, Europe had known many holy souls. Remote places in Africa and Asia had also witnessed the labors of saints. But what about the New World? Without doubt Archbishop Turribius, Francis Solano and Rose de Flores had done their part to serve God faithfully. Their lives had been given in atonement for the sins of those who had flocked westward in a wild search for wealth and power. But three saints, even three great saints, were not enough for the Western Hemisphere. Hundreds more were needed—men, women and children who knew how to love, who were not afraid to be victims for the wickedness of others.

"Lord, let me be one of these victims!" John begged. "Tell me what I should do to help my countrymen, then give me the strength to do it!"

So absorbed was the lay Brother in such thoughts that he failed to notice he had arrived at Santa Catalina, that the street was lined with carriages and that a great stream of people was moving into the public church attached to the monastery. A hand placed gently upon his shoulder was the final means of recalling him to himself.

"Brother John! Wake up!"

The gatekeeper turned around. A Negro of some forty-five years, dressed like himself in the black and white habit of the Dominican Order, was standing beside him and smiling in a friendly fashion.

Instantly John knew this was Brother Martin de
Porres, the holy religious of Santo Domingo who
was so loved by the poor and sick.

"Why, Brother Martin! I...I didn't expect to
meet you here!"

The Negro lay Brother smiled. "Father Prior told
me to come," he said. "You see, this is really a wonderful day for the Order, Brother John. The convent
for Dominican nuns which Rose de Flores prophe-
sied has become a reality at last."

John nodded, marveling all the while at his good
fortune in meeting Brother Martin. "It's early," he
said finally. "Maybe we have time for a little visit.
Dear Brother, I have so many things to ask you!"

Martin pointed to a side gate leading into the
monastery garden. "All right," he said. "I guess no
one will bother us if we go over there."

For half an hour the two sat together in the garden, heedless of the noise and clatter in the street
as fresh crowds arrived at Santa Catalina. With
childlike eagerness Martin listed the names of
friends for whom he wished prayers. Would John
ask God that such and such a man be cured of his
painful illness? That a certain woman be reunited
with her husband? That the required dowry be
found for a poor girl who wanted to enter a
convent?

"Of course I'll pray," said John, a bit overcome
that such a holy man as Martin should ask his
prayers. "But you must pray for my friends, too.
Dear Brother Martin! What crowds of poor are
coming to the Magdalena these days!"

MARTIN SMILED. "YES, LITTLE ROSE
OFTEN CAME TO VISIT ME."

A soft light stole into the Negro's eyes. "And we mustn't forget that each one represents Christ," he said gently. "Christ in America, dependent on our help! Giving us a chance to love Him in human beings like ourselves! Isn't it a wonderful thought?"

John nodded. "I wouldn't exchange my place as gatekeeper for all the wealth in the world!" he said fervently. "But tell me about this new convent, Brother. And about Rose de Flores. You knew her, didn't you?"

Martin smiled. "Yes, little Rose, *la Rosita*, often came to visit me. Ah, what a good child she was! Perhaps someday Americans will realize all she did for them by her prayers and sacrifices."

"Then you believe she'll be canonized?"

"Believe it? Brother John, I *know* it! In our own seventeenth century, Rose de Flores will be called 'Saint Rose of Lima'!"

Time passed and Martin continued his lavish praise of *la Rosita*. She had never been a nun but had reached perfection as a Dominican Tertiary. She had spent her lifetime of thirty-one years in prayer and penance for others. Among her great desires had been the erection of a Dominican convent for women in Lima—this very structure before them—where generous hearts could learn to love God as He wished to be loved.

"Several years before she died, the blessed child told her mother this monastery would be built," said Martin, "and that it would be dedicated to Saint Catherine of Siena. She also insisted that Doña Lucia de la Daga would provide the necessary funds and serve as the first Prioress. At the time Rose's mother had been furious. Doña Lucia was a happily married woman with five children. It did not seem fair to Don Antonio, her husband, to spread the rumor that his wife would end her days as a nun."

John smiled. "But Rose's words came true, Brother. I myself have heard how Doña Lucia's children died, one by one, and then her husband."

"That's right. And other prophecies also have come true. For instance, Rose's confessor, Father Luis de Bilbao, will say the first Mass in the new chapel this morning. And her mother, Maria Oliva de Flores, is now a Dominican Tertiary who tells everyone she is going to be a religious at Santa Catalina before very long."

John pondered these words silently. *Saint Rose of Lima!* How he wished he might have known this young sister in Saint Dominic! How ardently he would have asked her prayers, for himself and the poor folk who came to the Magdalena! Yet there was really no need to be sad because he could never see Rose with earthly eyes. The girl was now in Heaven. Like everyone else in that wonderful place, she could do much more for her friends than had ever been possible on earth. And why? Because at last she was one of those souls who had reached perfection—who had become worthy images of God Himself.

"Pray for me, little Rose," said John silently. "And for America, that many new saints will rise up here to love and praise God as you did."

CHAPTER 9

A FRIEND IN NEED

THE TWO lay Brothers spent a happy day together. From the newly dedicated monastery they went to Santo Domingo to pray before the last resting place of Rose de Flores. At the Franciscan church they venerated the remains of Father Francis Solano. After this they journeyed to the Cathedral where they knelt in meditation before the tomb of Archbishop Turribius. Then, realizing that John was supposed to be having a holiday, Martin suggested that they take a walk in the hills above the city. The air was good here and perhaps John would care to see the fig and olive trees he had planted for the poor?

For the rest of the day the two friends walked and talked in the quiet peace of the countryside. Below them stretched the great city of Lima, founded in 1535 by Don Francisco Pizarro—the city of gold and greed, of saints and suffering.

"Maybe someday this will be a place of pilgrimage," mused Martin, casting a fond glance on the city of his birth. "The good Archbishop Tur-

IT WAS TIME TO SAY GOODBYE. "MARTIN, YOU MUST
COME AND SEE ME SOON," SAID JOHN.

ribius lies buried here, Father Francis Solano, *la Rosita . . ."*

Doubtless another saint will be buried here, too," thought John. *"That will be you, good friend."* But he did not dare put such a thought into words. How embarrassed Martin would have been!

"Yes," he said softly. "Lima is a great city. I have found real happiness here."

The hours passed very quickly, and as the sun began to sink in the west, the two friends realized it was time to say good-bye. Because of the mountains that reared above the city, twilight was very brief. It would be dark in just a little while.

"You must come and see me soon," said John earnestly. "Will you promise to do that, Brother?"

Martin nodded. "I'll be glad to come on your next free day. That will be in four weeks' time?"

"That's right. On the tenth day of March. God be with you until then."

"And with you," replied Martin gratefully. "Don't forget to pray for my friends and me."

John smiled. "I won't forget. After all, it's little enough to do in return for all the happiness you've given me today."

After a few more words of farewell, the two friends parted company—Martin in a southerly direction, toward his home at Santo Domingo, John to the east and the monastery of the Magdalena. There was no real need for the latter to hurry, since his holiday would extend throughout the evening, but his step was rapid as he made his way across the city. He wanted to be home in time for the

Rosary said in common by the priests and Brothers. This beautiful prayer was still his favorite, and he never missed the public recitation if at all possible. However, he had gone but a short distance when his ears caught a pitiful sound. Someone, a child, was crying.

At once John stopped, while his eyes searched the darkness that was now filling the city streets. Who was in need? Some little Indian boy or girl? A Negro? Perhaps even the child of Spanish parents?

"Where are you, little one?" he called gently. "Don't be afraid. I've come to help you."

For a moment all was quiet. Then came a muffled sob and John realized that the object of his search was only a few feet away. Quickly he hurried forward and found a Negro boy of about nine years, thin beyond description and clothed in dirty rags, looking up at him fearfully from out the shadows of a deserted doorway.

As the lay Brother stretched out a friendly hand, the boy drew back. "Don't beat me!" he wailed. "I haven't done anything wrong. Honest!"

John smiled. "Of course not, little brother. But why aren't you home? It's getting too dark for children to be on the street."

The boy was sobbing again. "I haven't any home," he choked. "And I tried to beg today, at the new monastery, but the people never paid any attention! Oh, I'm so hungry! And tired!"

John was silent. Well he knew how extreme wealth and extreme poverty had existed side by side in Lima for almost a hundred years. Spanish nobles rode through the streets in golden carriages while Indians and Negroes, children like this one, died of neglect. Of course many of the ruling class were generous with alms. They gave money to the religious Orders so that the poor could be fed, widows and orphans housed in a fitting manner. But generally they stopped at this. They did nothing about changing the plight of the unfortunate, of providing opportunities for them to be independent of charity. Somehow they could not see that these poor people were meant to be their brothers in Christ, no matter what their color, their education, their intelligence. It was a real pity, for it meant that the wealthy Spaniards remained ignorant of one of the surest ways of pleasing God and becoming saints.

"What's your name?" asked John gently.

"Peter."

"You're baptized? You've heard about God?"

"No. . ."

The lay Brother took the boy's cold hand in his. "Well, come along and I'll tell you. And don't be afraid, Peter. You're going to have a good meal and some warm clothes in just a little while."

As the two made their way down the deserted street, very slowly, since the boy was weak from hunger, John suddenly remembered that there was no clothing at the Magdalena suitable for a youngster of Peter's size.

"I'll go in a store," he told himself. "Surely some merchant will be glad to help."

Unfortunately most of the shops where John was

known were closed. The dedication of the new monastery had caused a general holiday throughout the city, and the lay Brother found himself knocking in vain at one bolted door after another. Thus it was with a truly grateful heart that he finally came upon a large store that was still open. It belonged to a prosperous merchant, Don Francisco de Bustamante.

"Come along, Peter," said John kindly. "We'll get you some decent clothes in here."

The boy held back. "Don't make me go in that store," he begged. "*Please!*"

There was genuine dread in the lad's voice, and John was troubled. What was he going to do? He did not want to leave his young friend alone in the chilly street. And there would be no chance to get him suitable clothes if he did not go into the shop.

"Do you want to hide under my cloak?" he suggested. "That way no one will see you and you'd be quite warm."

The boy hesitated. Then a little smile brightened his thin face. "All right," he said, and crept gratefully beneath the folds of John's heavy black mantle.

Alas! Don Francisco de Bustamante was a hard-headed businessman. He had never heard of John Masias, gatekeeper of the Magdalena, and when the latter made his request for a suit of boy's clothes, likewise a donation for the poor, he let out a great roar.

"Are you crazy, Brother? I can't make any profit out of charity. And I've no time to talk to you just now. Can't you see I'm busy with my accounts?"

John's heart sank. "Surely you could spare a little something?" he ventured. "Some woolen material, perhaps? It wouldn't take much to clothe this boy."

The merchant peered across the counter. *"Boy?* What boy?"

John smiled and pulled aside his cloak. "This boy. His name is Peter."

As he looked at the frightened youngster before him, the man's face grew slowly white with rage. *"A Negro!"* he muttered unbelievingly. *"A Negro beggar in my store!"*

"A little child with an immortal soul," corrected John gently. "A little child who asks your help in God's Name. Surely you can't refuse him?"

With measured tread Don Francisco advanced from behind the counter. His eyes were blazing as he strode toward the door and threw it open. "Get out!" he hissed. "As for you, Brother, have more sense than to come here for alms again!"

Without a word John bowed humbly and guided his small companion back to the street. "Don't worry," he said, putting his arm about the child. "You'll be all right once we get to the monastery. And be sure of one thing, little friend. This merchant will never forget what happened tonight."

John's words proved true, for in the days that followed Don Francisco found himself in a strange predicament. Although the quality of his merchandise remained the same, the price and variety, no one came to buy. His regular customers took their trade to other stores without a word of explanation.

"I don't understand it," the anxious merchant

told a friend one morning. "Why, if this sort of thing keeps up, I'll be bankrupt in a year!"

The friend agreed and after some thought asked Don Francisco if he could remember who had entered his store last.

"Of course I remember," grumbled the merchant. "It was a Dominican lay Brother."

"You know his name?"

"Brother John Masias, the gatekeeper of the Magdalena."

"You were generous when he asked for alms?"

The merchant hesitated, then shook his head. "No, I told Brother John to leave my store and never to bother me again. You see, I was working on my accounts just then and charity was far from my thoughts. Besides, Brother John had a dirty little Negro with him who looked as though he would steal as soon as my back was turned. Why shouldn't I have told the two of them to get out?"

The friend was horrified at such a confession and speedily announced that Don Francisco's bad luck was due to the harsh treatment he had given a servant of God. "You'd better go to the Magdalena at once and ask his pardon," he said gravely. "Maybe the good Brother will take pity on you and ask God to send back your customers."

Don Francisco was not anxious to apologize, but the fear that soon he might have to sell his business drove him to conquer his natural feelings. With as much good grace as he could muster, he sought out John that same day and laid before him several lengths of good woolen cloth.

"For your poor," he said awkwardly, not daring to raise his eyes. "And forgive me for being rude the other night, Brother. It. . .it was very thoughtless of me."

A little smile curved the lay Brother's lips as he regarded the crestfallen merchant. "Thank you," he said gently. "This cloth is just what I needed. It will make several suits of clothes for my friends."

At these words fresh hope stirred in the visitor's heart. "Then you really do forgive me? You'll say some prayers for my. . .my success?"

John nodded. "I'll remember you, my friend. But not only that you may know success in business. I am going to ask God to give you the greatest grace of all."

Don Francisco looked up eagerly. "Yes?" he cried. "And what is that, Brother?"

"That you may save your soul. For if you lived to be a thousand years old, you could have no more important task than this."

The merchant was a little disappointed. He had hoped to hear that "the greatest grace of all" was something else. Health, perhaps. Or a high place in politics. But he dared make no complaint and thanked John as well as he could for his prayers and friendship.

"I'll come again," he promised. "And if you need anything, don't fail to count on me, Brother. After all, haven't I the best store in Lima?"

Brother John agreed, but his heart was sad as he watched his visitor depart. Already God had blessed Don Francisco in a material way. When he returned to his store, the contrite merchant would find his clerks overwhelmed with work. Once more the customers were on hand, in such huge numbers that they overflowed into the street.

"But he still doesn't understand the things a child should know," John told himself. "He hasn't really learned to love the poor—the Indians and Negroes—as he does himself. How I must pray for this unfortunate man!"

Late that night, as the gatekeeper knelt in solitary vigil before the Blessed Sacrament, he determined to recite an entire Rosary for Don Francisco de Bustamante. He set himself to the task with an eager heart, but he had not progressed very far in his prayer when a doleful sound caught his ear. It was soft and muffled, like the voices of distant mourners, and it seemed to come from the direction of the main altar.

John raised his eyes. The chapel was almost in darkness, save for the ruby glow of the sanctuary lamp and a few small candles that burned before the various shrines.

"Yes?" he whispered softly. "What is it? Who is there?"

Again came the mournful chorus, and presently John saw a number of shadowy figures advancing out of the darkness. Their eyes were filled with tears, their arms outstretched in desperate pleading. "Give us prayers!" they cried with one voice. "Oh, Brother John, you are the friend of the poor and sick! Be our friend, too! Help make us worthy to be with God and His blessed ones!"

The lay Brother stared in awe. Hundreds of men, women and children were grouped about the main altar. And every face was marked with loneliness and pain.

CHAPTER 10

NEW FRIENDS FOR JOHN

IT DID NOT take long to realize that the strangers were suffering souls from Purgatory. Through God's Mercy, John's human eyes were able to witness their pains, their great longing to enter Heaven without further delay.

"Dear friends, I'll try to help you," he said quickly. "I'll give you all the merits of my little prayers and sufferings."

At these words a muffled cry arose from the shadowy throng. "God bless you, Brother John!" came the grateful chorus. "And everyone else who remembers us!"

As time passed, the Brother recited the Rosary with even greater devotion. The Holy Souls continued to appear to him, and presently he noted that a wonderful change had come over one of the sufferers. Pain and loneliness had vanished from his face, and he was now bathed in a glorious light.

"His debt is paid!" thought John happily. "He's really worthy to enter Heaven now!"

The idea was so overwhelming that John could

not bring himself to end his prayers for the Poor Souls. One of these had just been made perfect, but how many millions remained who were still waiting for assistance, for the prayers and sacrifices that would enable them to purchase Heaven, too!

"Dear Lord, let many others understand about this," he pleaded. "Men and women and little children. Let them learn to think upon and love the Souls in Purgatory. After all, what can these poor creatures do for themselves? Time is no longer theirs. They cannot work or pray as they did while on earth. All they can do is suffer for the sins they were foolish enough to commit. And their suffering is so dreadful! There is nothing like it in the whole world!"

Very soon everyone at the Magdalena understood that Brother John was much in earnest about helping the Souls in Purgatory. Several times a day he sprinkled holy water on the ground, a practice which he insisted was of great help to the unseen sufferers. He also offered hundreds of short ejaculations as he went about his regular work, applying the merit of these little prayers to the Holy Souls. Then there was the greatest prayer of all—the Holy Sacrifice of the Mass. Not a day passed that John did not unite himself with the priest at the altar, begging the Heavenly Father to grant all sufferers eternal rest through the merits of Christ's death on Calvary.

"We can learn another lesson from our good friend," Father Gonzalez de Guzman told the community one day. "He is not only kind and thought-

ful to people in this world—the members of the
Church Militant. He also remembers the Church
Suffering—the millions of our brothers and sisters
in Purgatory. Because of this the saints in Heaven,
the members of the Church Triumphant, are only
too eager to help him all they can. Believe me, I
am beginning to learn the real meaning of charity
from Brother John."

Every listener was impressed by these words and
determined to imitate the gatekeeper as closely as
possible in his love for God and souls. The result
was a definite increase in virtue on the part of
everyone living at the Magdalena, noticeable in
only little things at first, then gradually reaching
greater proportions. As the years passed, there was
also another result. Fresh crowds came to the monastery with their trials and troubles, telling one
another it was the home of saints and of a lay
Brother who worked wonders for both rich and
poor.

Among these newcomers was Alonso Martin de
Orrelana. He had lived in Lima all his life, yet had
never grown wealthy as was the case with so many
other Spaniards. Now he hoped to change all this
by going to Spain and setting up a business for himself. First, however, he was determined to seek the
blessing of the lay Brother whose name was on
everyone's lips.

"My boat is leaving Callao in two days," he told
John eagerly. "Will you pray that I have a safe voyage, Brother? That I invest my little savings
wisely?"

Brother John gave a shrewd glance at the man before him. Alonso was in his early thirties, and it was quite evident he was an honest soul who was not afraid of hard work. And he was really setting great store on the proposed trip to Spain. Because of this, the Brother lost no time in giving what he knew to be good advice.

"Don't go on this trip," he advised. "It will only mean bad luck."

Alonso could scarcely believe his ears. Not take the trip, when he had worked for weeks to secure passage on the crowded boat? "I don't understand," he said lamely, the eagerness fading from his eyes. "Don Francisco de Bustamante is going. And many other important people. Surely it would be all right..."

A shadow crossed John's face. "You say Don Francisco is going?"

Alonso nodded. "Yes, Brother. And you know what a good head he has for business. I hope to get to know him on the trip and perhaps he'll introduce me to some of his wealthy friends in Spain. You see, if I can just make some good connections..."

Again John shook his head. "Cancel your passage," he ordered. "And tell Don Francisco to do the same. Give him my message this very day."

At these words Alonso's happiness vanished entirely. He tried to explain his plan again but the words stuck in his throat. Seeing his disappointment, John reached out a comforting hand. "Don't be unhappy," he urged. "If you want to make a good living, invest your money here in Lima. Buy a little shop and open a bakery. Then see how your luck will change."

The Brother's words were occasion for fresh distress on Alonso's part. A *bakery?* Why, he knew nothing about running such a place! Surely it would be better to go to Spain with Don Francisco and the other important people. Yet he made no comment. After all, he had come to the Magdalena for just one reason: to obtain the blessing of John Masias on his approaching trip. Well, Brother John would not give such a blessing. For some strange reason he thought Alonso should be a baker.

"Pray for me, Brother!" cried the unhappy man suddenly. "The Devil is trying so hard to make me go against your wishes!"

John smiled. Well he knew the struggle that was taking place in his friend's heart. "I'll pray for you," he said quickly. "The one thing I ask is that you go at once to Don Francisco and warn him against the trip. Will you do this?"

The man sighed. "All right," he said slowly. "If that's the way you want it, Brother."

Strangely enough, Alonso's feeling of depression vanished entirely as he walked the short distance to Don Francisco's shop. When he arrived with John's message, he could even laugh about his recent disappointment and wonder why he had not thought of being a baker before. After all, his wife Gertrude was a good cook, and people had to eat. There was no reason why the two of them could not start a really fine bakeshop. It would be on a

small scale at first, of course, with just bread and
plain cakes, but later it could branch out with fan-
cier wares to catch the better trade.

"I'll go and tell Gertrude about it right now!"
he thought excitedly. "She'll be so pleased!" But he
resolutely put aside the tempting notion as he
recalled John's parting words: *"Go at once to Don
Francisco and warn him against the trip."*

"May Heaven help me to speak up well!" he
thought. "I'm sure Don Francisco will have good
luck, too, if only he listens to Brother John's
advice."

At the very moment when Alonso was entering
the prosperous merchant's store, prepared to carry
out his assignment, another problem was being
presented to John at the Magdalena. This time his
visitor was Captain Michael de Espina, who had
come to talk about his two boys, Anthony and Luis.

"I've prayed for years that the lads would have
religious vocations," the Captain told John anxiously. "Now I think God has heard part of my
prayer, for Anthony says he wants to come here to
the Magdalena to study for the priesthood. But
Luis. . .oh, dear!"

John smiled. "I take it Luis is causing you
concern?"

"*Concern?* Brother, that's hardly the word. He
won't study. He roams the streets with worthless
companions. He's untidy about his clothes. And
there's nothing anyone can do about it. He just
laughs when we scold him and goes off about his
own business—whatever that is. Why, just now I

spied the young rascal climbing in your orchard. And he had five other boys with him. If you want to save your orange trees..."

There was a little smile on John's lips as he listened to the long account of Luis' faults. Deep in his heart he felt that the boy was not wicked, only lacking in judgment and experience. But he could appreciate the Captain's concern. The poor man was really worried that someday this youngest son would do something to disgrace his family's good name.

"I wouldn't worry too much about Luis," he said finally. "Perhaps if I go down to the orchard and say a few words..."

The Captain sighed. "The lad needs more than words, Brother John. His mother could tell you that much. And his sister Beatrice."

"Well, prayers then. And by the way, how old is Luis?"

The Captain sighed again, even more deeply this time. "Thirteen, Brother. And if you were in my shoes, you'd agree that is the worst possible age for a boy."

John checked a great desire to laugh, gravely assuring the worried Captain he would speak to Luis. Then he bade his new friend a kindly farewell and asked Brother Dionysius to take charge of the gate for a little while. He himself was going down to the orchard.

It did not take long to reach it, for the orange trees belonging to the Magdalena were only a block away. As he pushed open the wooden gate, John could hear the excited laughter of Luis and his companions as they climbed up and down one tree and then another.

"What shall I say to the boys?" he thought anxiously. "Dear Lord, please give me the right words!"

The right words were not long in coming, or the chance to say them, for as they caught sight of the lay Brother in his black and white habit, Luis and his friends halted abruptly in their play.

"We'd better get out of here," said one of them quickly. "That Brother may be angry."

Luis de Espina laughed. "We haven't hurt anything," he said. "Besides, what can a lay Brother do to us? He's only a servant to the priests. Come on, let's see what he wants."

So the boys started down the orchard to meet John, a bit fearfully, save for young Luis. He was quite prepared to laugh off all threats and scoldings as he did at home. And just to prove his courage, he seized an orange from a low-hanging branch and began to peel it with carefree impudence.

"Hello, Brother," he said cheerfully. "Isn't it a nice day?"

John smiled. "Yes, it's a beautiful day," he said, calmly seating himself on a nearby bench.

The boys stared. Was this all? Wasn't the lay Brother going to scold them for playing in the orchard? As the minutes passed, even Luis began to wonder. Surely this Brother was going to do something else than just sit and smile.

"Did you want something?" he asked finally.

"Would you like us to help you pick some oranges?"

John shook his head. "No, thanks, boys. But I do have a little problem. I've been thinking about it for some time and maybe you could help me. You see, I'm worried about a young friend of mine."

Luis pricked up his ears. "Young? How young, Brother?"

"Oh...I guess he's about thirteen."

"Why, that's my age!"

"*Really?*"

"Yes. I was born in 1624 and this is 1637. My name is Luis de Espina, in case you're interested."

John seemed very much pleased with this information. "You were born in 1624," he mused. "That's wonderful, Luis. And how old will you be in 1724?"

By now the boys had forgotten their previous fears and were gathered close about John. This question made all of them laugh. "He won't even be living," said one of them. "He'll be dead by that time."

Luis looked at his half-eaten orange. "I will, too," he said defiantly. "I'll be a hundred years old."

"All right. And how old will you be in 1824?"

At this even Luis had to smile. He could not see himself living for two hundred years.

"I'll be dead by 1824," he admitted. "Dead and buried."

"And your soul?"

The boy laughed awkwardly. "Why I guess it will be in Heaven, Brother."

"You're sure? You're working hard to make it worthy?"

By now six pairs of young eyes were fixed on John in puzzled concern. With a gentle smile he rose to his feet. "Don't be so serious, boys. I only asked a simple question. You see, I find it rather nice to think about the future sometimes, about the years 1724 and 1824 and so on. I ask myself if I am doing my duty now, as well as I can, so that those years will find me happy with God. It's a good habit, I think."

Seeing that Luis and his companions were a trifle embarrassed, the lay Brother had a happy thought. Would the boys like to come to the kitchen for a little lunch? And a look about the monastery? At these words the youngsters relaxed.

"We'd like that a lot, Brother," said Luis. "And maybe...that is, if it's all right..."

"Yes?" prompted John. "What else can I do for you?"

The boy grinned shyly. "I'd like to see your room," he said. "You know, the place where you sleep."

A few minutes later John was escorting his young friends through the silent corridors of the monastery. There was an amused smile on his face as he stopped outside his little cell. "There's not much to see in here," he announced. "Look for yourself, Luis."

The boy pushed open the door. John's cell was a very tiny room with just one window. A bed made of planks stood against one wall. It had no mattress

Dearest Mother I
have brought you
some new
children

JOHN KNELT DOWN AND BEGAN TO PRAY ALOUD.

or sheets, only a worn grey blanket for covering. A few feet away stood the large chest containing assorted clothing for the poor. The remaining furniture consisted of a chair and table.

The boys were silent as they looked about. Suddenly Luis touched John's arm. "What's that?" he asked curiously. "That picture over your bed with the light before it?"

John's eyes widened. "Why, that's Our Lady with the Christ Child, Luis. Surely you knew that!"

The boy reddened. "I'm sorry. I thought it was some saint."

"It is a saint," said the lay Brother gently. "The greatest of all God's creatures. She's my best friend and yours. She gives me everything I ask."

The boy looked intently at the picture. It was a small one, painted on linen, and in places the colors were dim and faded. "*She* gives you everything you ask?" he whispered incredulously.

John nodded. "Everything. When I run out of food and clothing for the poor, I come here and ask her help. In a little while some good soul arrives at the gate with the very things I needed. Ah, Luis, the Mother of God is a wonderful friend!"

For several minutes the boys stood looking at the picture. There was something about the little image that attracted them. Our Lady's face was so kind and understanding. It almost seemed as though she was pleased that six boys had come to visit her.

Suddenly John knelt down. To his young friends' great astonishment, he began to pray aloud, and in words that concerned each of them directly.

"Dearest Mother, I've brought you some new children," he whispered, "children who want to know and love your Son. Will you teach them? And will you give them the grace to be very holy some day?"

CHAPTER 11

THE DOOR TO JOY

IN THE WEEKS that followed, several families in Lima noted a remarkable change taking place in their young sons. The boys were now much interested in school work, particularly in Latin. They arose early in the morning and assisted at Mass. They were respectful to parents and teachers, no longer roaming the streets in idle groups or getting into mischief. Indeed, it seemed as though a real miracle had taken place, and the families gave due thanks for the wonderful favor. However, when the boys presently announced that they wanted to study for the priesthood, their parents grew a little worried. This was almost too much. What could have happened?

Captain Michael de Espina asked himself this same question many times, and with good reason. Luis, who had caused friends and family so much concern, was among the boys so strangely converted. More than that. The lad insisted he would join his brother Anthony at the Magdalena. The life there was difficult, but it was the life he wanted.

"John Masias must have had a hand in this," the Captain told himself. "I'm going to ask him if it isn't so."

It was around noon when Captain Michael arrived at the monastery, and as usual the place was crowded with beggars. Brother Dionysius de Vilas, John's assistant, was feeding a number of them at the gate, but of John himself there was no evidence. The Captain was not worried, however. He knew from experience that his good friend would be inside the monastery, dispensing charity to poor priests and others who did not wish to be seen begging in public.

As was his custom at such times, the Captain went through a side door which the lay Brother had given him permission to use, and then sat down to wait in a small hallway. Very soon he grew impatient, however, and started off in the direction where he knew John to be.

"It won't take long to ask him about Luis," he thought. "Dear God, I can hardly believe that my little boy wants to be a Dominican! And here at the Magdalena, of all places!"

As the Captain was about to enter the private room where John was ministering to his special guests, he stopped abruptly. A few yards away a little group of needy was seated at a long wooden table. Everything was neat and clean, and happiness was on each face. Yet it was not this which made Captain Michael stare. It was the sight of the good Brother kneeling before an old priest and filling his plate with nourishing food, then moving to the next guest and repeating the action.

"He doesn't have to kneel like this," thought the Captain. "He really doesn't." Then suddenly he remembered a previous conversation he had had with John. At that time the lay Brother had explained his reason for feeding the poor on his knees. When people came to him for help, John did not see just a needy man or woman. He saw Christ.

"That's why I kneel before my poor friends," he had said simply. "I feel as though I were before the Tabernacle."

Remembering these words, the Captain forgot his previous impatience and withdrew to the hallway. In a few minutes John came to him here and the father had a chance to tell his surprising news. The lay Brother listened in silence, a slow smile lighting up his face as he heard of Luis' desire to enter the Magdalena.

"That's wonderful," he said quietly. "Oh, my friend, how good God is to those who ask His help!"

The Captain nodded. "But you had something to do with this, Brother. Come now. Isn't that so?"

John lowered his eyes. "I did ask Our Lady to make your boy holy someday. And his friends. But it was not my prayers that worked this wonder, Captain Michael. It was the grace of God."

The Captain grew thoughtful. "At least you can help me on one score." he said. "Do you think Luis is being led away by. . .well, by youthful enthusiasm? After all, he's only thirteen. It may be the lad won't persevere in his good intentions. Perhaps

I should make him wait a while before starting his studies for the priesthood."

John shook his head. "Oh, no!" he cried quickly. "Never put an obstacle in the way of a religious vocation, Captain. So often it spoils everything for young souls who want to give themselves to God."

"But the life at the Magdalena is so hard, Brother! You know that yourself. The fasts, the long prayers, the study. My Luis isn't used to any of these things."

John smiled. "I'll watch out for him," he said. "After all, students who are only thirteen are excused from a number of our difficult practices so there's no real need to worry. Just go in peace, Captain, and thank God for the wonderful grace He has given your family."

When Captain Michael finally took his departure, John made his way to the monastery gate, where nearly one hundred Indians and Negroes were waiting for him. Their physical hunger was now satisfied, and it was time to satisfy another hunger—that of their souls. For almost an hour the little group listened attentively as John explained the truths contained in the Catechism. A glimmer of new hope shone in their eyes as they listened to their favorite story—an explanation of the meaning of Baptism.

John's face was radiant as he told his friends how the Sacrament of Baptism had made them children of God. Although they were poor now, and looked down upon by the leaders of their country, they were really very dear to the Heavenly Father. A time would come, if they were faithful in keeping the Commandments, when all injustice would be at an end. Then they would find themselves heirs to everlasting happiness. Billions of saints would recognize them as brothers. The dreadful prejudice against race and color would be ended forever.

After he had finished his talk, John went to the chapel. It was his custom to spend two hours here every afternoon, telling his problems to Our Lord in the Blessed Sacrament. This time was very dear to him. All the trials and troubles brought him by his friends were now laid before Our Lord. In the manner of a little child, John asked for guidance.

Such and such a man might be in business difficulties or ill. "Please help him, dear Lord!" the gatekeeper would plead. "And even if You sent him these trials because of his sins, won't You be merciful? Let me suffer for him instead!"

John's prayers were not always prayers of petition. Every day he gave thanks, too. Just recently, for instance, there was new cause for rejoicing. Alonso Martin de Orrelana, the honest soul who had wanted to seek his fortune in Spain, had listened to John instead. Now he and his wife were doing very well with a little bakeshop.

"Thank You for being kind to Alonso," thought John. "Dear God, continue to bless this friend of mine. And his wife."

As he prayed for the baker, John was not unmindful of another acquaintance. This was Don Francisco de Bustamante, the wealthy merchant who had also wanted to go to Spain. Alas! He had paid no attention to John's warnings, and a few days ago word had reached Lima that his ship had run into a terrible storm. It had broken into pieces off the coast of Panama, and all lives were lost.

"Give the poor man eternal rest!" John begged. Then, realizing that Don Francisco had been very far from being a saint, that he had never really learned to think of the unlettered Indians and Negroes as his brothers, he added a familiar plea. "If Don Francisco is in Purgatory, let me take his sufferings for myself, Lord. Let me make up for his sins."

As time passed and John lost himself in prayers for his friends, a remarkable thing happened. God set aside the laws of nature and allowed the body of the humble lay Brother to rise into the air until it was on a level with a large crucifix near the altar. Such a miracle was once witnessed by a number of priests and Brothers who had come to the chapel for private prayer of their own. Everyone was struck dumb with reverence save Father Francis de Avendaño, an elderly priest who had never appreciated John's extraordinary closeness to God.

"I'm going to see Father Prior about this!" he sputtered after the little group had stepped outside the chapel. "There's really no need to have these...these acrobatics! And right in the sanctuary, too! Why can't Brother John act like the rest of us?"

The other priests and Brothers did not know what to say. After all, Father Francis was older and they owed him respect. But one Brother did make an effort to defend the gatekeeper.

"Brother John's a saint!" he whispered in an awed voice. "Father, just look now! His face is shining like the sun!"

Father Francis cast a brief glance toward the altar. Brother John was still floating in the air, his arms outstretched to the crucifix. There was a soft light playing about his whole body, but the priest dismissed the wonder with a wave of his hand.

"I haven't any use for a ridiculous display like this," he declared. "I'm quite sure that Brother John is a saint, as you say, but I still see no reason for him to float about in the air. After all, some of our young religious may be affected by this in the wrong way. They'll think they aren't pleasing to God unless they float through the air, too. When they don't, they'll become discouraged and maybe some of them will even leave the Order."

A murmur of astonishment ran through the little group. "Oh, no!" cried one young priest. "It couldn't happen like that, Father!"

"And why not?"

"Because Brother John wouldn't let it."

Father Francis folded his arms beneath his long white scapular. "That's what you think. But I think it's my duty to speak to Father Prior and ask him to put a stop to all such exhibitions. Brother John will have to obey *him*."

The Prior listened patiently when the elderly priest arrived with his complaints. However, he did not seem to think that John's ecstasies were harming any of the younger religious. After all, everyone knew that the gatekeeper was one of God's chosen friends. Like Martin de Porres, the holy Brother at Santo Domingo, his extraordinary graces were for the good of other souls as well as his own.

"I guess I don't think it necessary to order Brother John to change his ways," he said kindly. "If he prays with such love as to cause his body to rise above the earth, well—let us rejoice, Father. We have a saint in our midst."

"Then you don't think his visions will make Brother John proud?"

The Prior laughed. "Father Francis, I give you permission to scold Brother John any time you think he is suffering from pride. Mark my words. He'll receive the correction as though it were a great gift."

Father Francis had to be content with this, and for the next few days watched for an opportunity to catch the lay Brother in some fault. All such efforts were to little avail, however. Brother John never broke the Rule, even slightly. He was on time for all the community prayers; he kept silence; he fulfilled his duty to the poor and needy to perfection. He was kind, cheerful, willing.

Father Francis did not give up hope, however, and finally came the opportunity for which he had waited so long. Late one night young Luis de Espina, who recently had been clothed in the Dominican habit, was sent to the chapel to find a book for the Novice Master. The fourteen-year-old lad was fearful, for he knew that the body of a dead man was lying in the darkened sanctuary. It was that of Don Pedro de Castilla, one of the monastery's great benefactors, whose funeral would take place the next day.

Young Luis had never seen a dead man, nor did he want to see one now. His whole being cringed at the thought of having to enter the empty chapel and look for the book in question. Yet what could he do? He had come to the Magdalena in order to study for the priesthood, and he realized that as a religious obedience would always be his most important task. Right now it was even more important than doing well with his studies.

With a little prayer for help, Luis lighted a candle and started on his mission. The dark corridors were deserted, for it was not quite time for Matins, and most of the friars were still asleep. As the boy finally reached the door leading to the sanctuary, he paused fearfully. What should he do now? Say some more prayers? Or just take a deep breath, walk firmly into the sanctuary and start to hunt for the book?

With trembling hands Luis pushed open the door and peered into the shadows. All was quiet in the sanctuary, but the boy shivered as his glance fell upon a long narrow object near the foot of the altar steps. Yes—it was a magnificent ebony coffin, with six tall candles glimmering about it! And in the coffin, resplendent in his royal robes of office, was Don Pedro de Castilla!

For a moment Luis stared at the corpse. Then he crept forward cautiously. *The book, where could it be?* But he had not progressed far with his search when his heart froze anew. He was not alone in the chapel! Someone, something, had just moved! Half paralyzed with dread, the boy lifted his candle and peered into the shadows. As he did so, he caught sight of a white-clad figure just above his head. It was too dark to make out the face but the feet were plainly visible. Two feet, standing on nothing but air!

For several seconds Luis stared silently at the floating figure. Then his fear found words. *"A ghost!"* he shrieked. *"Don Pedro's ghost!"*

A sudden draft blew out the candle in his hand, and for a brief space the boy staggered. Then he crumpled in a heap on the rough stone floor. Once again all was quiet in the sanctuary, but now the tall funeral candles cast their flickering rays over two lifeless figures: Don Pedro in his coffin and a child novice in his rumpled white habit.

Help was not long in coming. Luis' terrified cries had been heard by several friars who were on their way to the chapel for private prayer before Matins. When they reached the boy's side, they questioned him anxiously, heedless of the fact that it was the time of the "Great Silence."

"What is it?" cried one. "What happened, Brother Luis?"

But the lad did not move, and soon everyone realized that young Luis de Espina was unconscious. The only thing to do was to carry him to the infirmary and call a doctor. So the little procession set out, slowly and carefully, every heart concerned with one question: what had caused this healthy boy to faint?

It was almost an hour before the young novice could give a satisfactory answer, and then it was Father Francis de Avendaño who brought this about. Luis had seen a figure floating in the air, hadn't he? Near the crucifix above the main altar? It was this that had frightened him?

"I saw two feet," whispered the boy weakly. "It was...the dead man..."

"Nonsense!" declared Father Francis. "You saw Brother John Masias in one of his ecstasies, that's all. Ah, just wait until Father Prior hears the truth about this! Maybe he'll remember my warning."

The Prior did remember Father Francis' warning and accordingly sent for John without delay. "Our Brother Luis is very ill," he said severely. "You gave him a dreadful shock last night, Brother John, and I only hope you have a good excuse."

There were tears in the gatekeeper's eyes as he prostrated himself at the Prior's feet. "I haven't any excuse, Father. Please tell me what I must do."

For a moment the Prior was silent, visibly touched by the lay Brother's genuine sorrow. It was going to be hard to punish a holy man like Brother John, but after all, duty was duty. "You will eat nothing but bread and water for a week," he said sternly. "And that's not all. In the future you'll be locked in the chapel each night so that none of the other Brothers can go there and be frightened out of their wits. Now be off with you. And say some prayers for poor Brother Luis. The lad's nerves are in a dreadful condition."

"WHY WERE YOU SO FRIGHTENED?"
JOHN ASKED GENTLY.

With heavy heart John obeyed his superior's command, not because of the severe penance just given to him but because he felt he had failed in charity to another human being.

"I must go and see Luis," he told himself. "Poor little boy! I owe him far more than an ordinary apology."

So after due thought and prayer, John went to the infirmary to do what he could for his young friend. He found the boy still white and shaken, but without ill feelings toward him.

"Why were you so frightened?" Brother John asked gently. "Didn't you know me in the sanctuary last night?"

The boy shook his head. Then he shyly told the gatekeeper of his great secret. He was terrified of corpses, of coffins, of graves—of everything pertaining to death. It was really Don Pedro who was responsible for his present illness, not John. A smile crossed the latter's face as he listened to his young friend's words.

"But why be afraid of death?" he said kindly. "There's no need for that, Luis. And as for a grave—do you know what it really is?"

The boy shivered. "A grave is where they put dead people," he whispered. "Please let's not talk about graves, Brother."

"A grave is the door to joy," said John gently. "You must remember that, little brother. *The door to joy!*"

For the next few minutes the gatekeeper spoke so glowingly of death, of the beauties to which it led, that the young novice was drawn out of his fear. He had never heard death described in such fashion before. Why, it was a wonderful thing, particularly for a religious! It meant the beginning of the reward given by God to all those who had left parents, friends and the good things of life for His sake.

"In a year's time you will hear of a really wonderful death," said John slowly. "A saint will die in Lima, little brother, and you and I will witness some of his miracles."

Luis' eyes widened. "*A saint?*" he whispered. "Who is it, Brother John? And when will he die?"

The gatekeeper smiled. "Can you remember this date, Luis? November 3, 1639?"

The boy nodded. Of course he could remember November 3, 1639. But who was going to die on that day? Who was the person Brother John believed to be a saint?

CHAPTER 12

JOHN TAKES A REST

IN DUE COURSE the two questions were
answered. On the date mentioned by John,
Brother Martin de Porres went to receive his
heavenly reward. He was sixty years old, and there
was not a soul in Lima who did not feel he was
a saint. Those who had known him personally realized their good fortune and congratulated themselves upon it. Those who had never met the Negro
lay Brother were determined to get at least one
look at him before he was buried. They flocked to
his former home at Santo Domingo, confident that
he would intercede for them with God. Such great
faith was wonderfully rewarded, for before long
even the dust from Martin's tomb was working
miracles. It was impossible to keep track of the
many invalids who had been cured by its pious use.

John was delighted at the great honor being paid
his old friend, not only because it was a well-
merited reward but because it meant an increase
in virtue for so many people. The thousands of
prayers offered in Martin's honor could never go

without result. Even when the various petitions were seemingly ignored, God's graces were flooding the souls of those who prayed.

"It's the same with every prayer," John thought. "There is always an answer on God's part. What a pity that so many people never think of this! If they did, they would spend far more time on their knees. And they wouldn't feel so disappointed when the little favors they ask are not granted. They would realize far better things are being given them by God's Providence."

Occasionally Father Gonzalez de Guzman succeeded in getting John to put a little of such wisdom into words. The priest was the lay Brother's confessor and had considerable authority over him. John was never anxious to tell of his inner life, but he knew the merit of obedience, and the questions asked by Father Gonzalez were always promptly answered. However, one day these questions caused more than ordinary embarrassment, for the priest arrived to speak with John at ten o'clock in the morning.

Now ten o'clock in the morning was a rather important hour for the lay Brother. At this time the donkey owned by the monastery (but committed to the care of Brother John) was due to return from a solitary begging trip about the city. When the little beast was in its awkward youth, Brother John, despairing of its stubbornness, had asked Saint John the Evangelist to make the creature useful. Saint John had answered his prayer generously, teaching the donkey not only to permit the baskets to be tied to his back but to go of his own accord from house to house, begging. But Father Gonzalez did not know this, so that he was really startled when, looking through the open window to identify a sharp sound, he saw the donkey striking the monastery gate with one hoof.

"Why, it's the donkey!" he cried. "When did he learn that?"

Brother John could hardly suppress a smile. "Ah, years ago. He's a very wonderful fellow. You must know him better. And now, if you will excuse me, I must let him in for his drink of water and his apple. He has worked hard this morning."

"Worked hard? What do you mean?"

Brother John looked out to where the little donkey stood watching the latch expectantly. "See his baskets, Father? They are full of gifts that good souls have sent me for the poor."

The priest sat in utter astonishment as Brother John bowed himself out of the room. When he returned some minutes later, he was ready with a number of questions: "You don't mean that this little animal goes out begging *alone?*"

"Oh, yes, Father. Everyone knows him."

"Has anyone ever tried to steal from his baskets?"

Brother John flushed with amusement at the memory, picturing the donkey's great eyes, full of the most solemn innocence. "Well, yes, Father. And I'm afraid that he behaved in every way unbefitting the donkey of a Dominican monastery. Kicked and bit, I was told. But then, Father, what can you expect of the beast of so weak and imperfect a master?"

"Go on," said Father Gonzalez, resigning himself to accept without further question another of Brother John's miracles. "Tell me some of the places where the donkey goes."

"Alonso Martin, the baker, is always very generous," said John eagerly. "The good soul has done very well with his bakeshop, Father. He sends me bread every day in the donkey's baskets. Then there is Doctor Carrasco. And Anthony de Alarcon..."

"*Anthony de Alarcon!*" cried the priest. "I'd almost forgotten, John. He's the real reason I came to speak with you this morning. Now—can you guess why?"

The lay Brother nodded. "The poor soul wants me to pray about his deafness, Father. And I have prayed. But his cure won't come for some time yet. I wish he could understand that just now it's God's Will that he bear this trouble patiently."

"Oh, so he is going to be cured someday?"

"Yes, Father."

"When?"

Again confusion crept into the lay Brother's eyes. "Anthony will be cured after my death," he said slowly. "You...you can tell him that if you wish, Father. The time isn't too far away."

Now it was the priest's turn to be confused. "*John!* You know you're not going to die for a long time yet!"

A slow smile crossed the gatekeeper's face. "I have only six years left in which to serve God," he said softly. "I shall die at the age of sixty, Father, the same age as good Brother Martin de Porres."

For a moment Father Gonzalez shifted uncomfortably. John had been right about so many things. Could he be right about this, too? Suddenly he leaned toward the lay Brother, a serious look on his face.

"You have a great love for the Blessed Mother, haven't you, John? She speaks to you sometimes?"

The gatekeeper nodded slowly. "Oh, yes, Father. Our Lady's picture in my cell. . .it has. . .well, *lived* for me over and over again."

"And her statue in the Rosary chapel? What about that?"

John smiled. It was quite evident that Father Gonzalez was in a questioning mood today. "I know what you want to hear, Father," he said slowly. "It's about last week, isn't it? Well, I'll tell you. It won't take very long."

Satisfied, Father Gonzalez settled himself to listen to his good friend, marveling at how like a child the man before him was. John always spoke so simply of the most wonderful things.

"It was midnight, Father, when you and the others were reciting Matins in church," began the lay Brother. "I was not far away, for you know I like to be in choir at Office time whenever I can."

The priest nodded. "Yes, John, although it might be better for you to be resting. But go on."

"Well, I was in the Rosary chapel praying before Our Blessed Lady's statue when suddenly there was a strange creaking in the walls and floor. Some vases of flowers overturned on the altar, and right away. . ."

"And right away you knew it was an earthquake," put in Father Gonzalez. "Ah, John, we do have so many earthquakes in Lima! And they cause such suffering and destruction! Why is it? How can God allow such terrible things to happen?"

The lay Brother looked up in genuine surprise. "Why? Because it's His Will," he said.

The priest pretended to be dissatisfied with such an answer. "You mean that God *wants* people to suffer? That He really enjoys seeing souls in pain?"

John shook his head. "Oh, no!" he cried. "God is wonderfully kind and good. But sometimes He sends suffering because that is the only way to make certain people turn to Him."

"Oh," said Father Gonzalez. "Now I understand. But finish your story, Brother. I didn't mean to interrupt."

"The priests stopped their prayers when the walls and ceiling began to shake, for they were afraid that the church would fall down on them. A number rushed out to the garden. . ."

"Including myself."

"Yes, Father. And I would have run out there, too, only suddenly I heard a voice tell me to stay where I was. It came from Our Lady's statue."

"Yes?" prompted the older religious. "And what did the statue say?"

There was a look of childlike simplicity in John's eyes as he began to recall the latest wonder in his life. "I heard Our Lady say these words: *'Brother*

John, my little friend, why are you running away?
Don't you see that I am here to watch over you?"

Father Gonzalez leaned forward eagerly. "Yes?
And what else did Our Lady say, Brother?"

The latter smiled. "She spoke no more, Father.
But when I looked up at the statue it was shining
like the sun. I forgot all about the earthquake then
and stayed where I was. Somehow I don't think I'll
ever be afraid of earthquakes again."

For a moment the priest was silent, lost in admiration at the wonder just related to him. Then he
got to his feet. "I guess I'll be going now," he said.
"Thank you, Brother, for the things you've told me.
And remember to say a little prayer for me each
day, won't you?"

The lay Brother nodded. "I always pray for my
friends," he said. "It's a real privilege."

As the weeks passed, John's reputation for sanctity increased even more, and presently he was
involved in a new wonder. This concerned a young
Negro named Anthony who had been working as
part-time helper at the gate. The lad was devoted
to John and willingly served him in a variety of
ways. One day, however, while drawing water from
the well, Anthony lost his footing and fell. His cries
attracted the attention of Brother John of the
Rosary, an Indian, who did his best to help the boy,
but to no avail. In desperation, the young religious
ran to the gatekeeper to tell him of the tragedy.

"I found a rope but it was too short!" he cried.
"Oh, Brother John, what are we going to do?"

Strangely enough, the gatekeeper did not seem

at all interested in Anthony's plight. "Can't you see I'm busy?" he told the newcomer. "A poor old lady just came for a meal. I must attend to her first."

All the more terrified at the amazing reply, the young Indian hurried off to find other help, and on his way met Luis de Espina, now fully recovered from his illness. With frantic haste he urged Luis to try to make Brother John understand. But the gatekeeper would not listen to Luis, either. Instead, he continued to minister to the old lady, and only after half an hour did he finally appear at the well. He found a group of religious gathered here, bowed with grief.

"Well," he asked gently, "why do you all look so sad? What's happened?"

John of the Rosary and Luis de Espina could scarcely believe their ears. "We told you!" they cried with one voice. "Anthony fell in the well half an hour ago. Oh, Brother John! Why didn't you come and save him?"

John smiled. "You are very fearful, little brothers. Didn't you know that Anthony would be quite all right without me?"

Young Luis was almost in tears. "He's drowned now. We've called and called but there's no reply. And look at the rope, Brother John! It just hangs into the water. It doesn't move!"

Quickly the gatekeeper made his way to the well and peered into the dark opening. "Anthony, my son! Answer me! Are you all right?"

A murmur of astonishment ran through the crowd. Surely Brother John didn't think the boy still alive! Why, the well was thirty feet deep, and the stone sides were far too slippery for anyone to gain a foothold.

"We may be able to reach the body if we get some iron hooks," suggested a young priest hurriedly. "It's the only thing left to do."

At these words John held up a warning hand. "Sssh!" he whispered. "Listen!"

The priests and Brothers crowded closer about the well. Suddenly a chill of fear and joy ran through the little group as a voice was heard echoing in the dark depths. They strained to listen.

"Brother John," the cry came, faintly, "when are you going to take me out of here? This water is so cold!"

Half beside himself with joy, Luis de Espina grasped John's arm. "It's Anthony!" he cried. "He's alive!"

"Of course he's alive," said the gatekeeper cheerfully. "Now, take hold of the rope and we'll bring him up."

Within half an hour the story of the young Negro's remarkable rescue was making the rounds in Lima. Crowds flocked to the Magdalena, eager to hear the wonder from the boy's own lips and to look once more on the holy lay Brother whose prayers could work such miracles. But although young Anthony told everything he knew, including the almost unbelievable fact that the Blessed Virgin herself had held his head above the water, there was no trace of John. He had hidden himself in a remote corner of the monastery.

Father Gonzalez de Guzman wrote down the details of this latest wonder in a little book. "It may come in useful," he told the Prior, Father Blaise de Acosta. "You see, something tells me our Brother John will be canonized someday. Perhaps in company with his old friend, Brother Martin de Porres."

The Prior agreed. "That was really a wonderful partnership," he mused. "A Negro and a white man, both offering themselves as victims for sinners—for America. Ah, Father, the stories of these two good souls ought to be known by everyone!"

Father Gonzalez smiled. "They will be known someday," he said. "I'm quite sure of it." Then, after a moment's hesitation, he informed the superior that John did not think he would stay on earth much longer.

"He keeps telling me that he will live to be Martin's age, Father—sixty years. No more, no less. Well, I'm afraid we ought to believe what he says since he's always been right about future events."

A shadow crossed the Prior's face. *"John is going to die?* Oh, no, Father! Not for a long time. Why, he's in very good health these days."

"Yes—but there are his works of penance, Father Prior. He performs so many of them. I think in the end they will cause his death."

Father Gonzalez was right. In late August of the year 1645, Brother John Masias grew noticeably thin and pale. He was ordered to take better care of himself and to let Brother Dionysius, his assistant, handle most of his duties. The gatekeeper protested that he was quite well, but the word of the

Prior prevailed. There was to be no more fasting on bread and water; no more vigils in the chapel at night. For once John was to treat his body with care and attention.

The faithful lay Brother obeyed his superior's order, but with great reluctance. What was the use of taking a rest now? In a short while he would be dead and no amount of sleep, food or medicine could alter the fact.

"I will go to God on the eighteenth day of September," he told himself happily. "Ah, what a wonderful day that will be!"

Presently, with the simplicity of a little child, he sought out his old friend and guide, Father Gonzalez de Guzman. "I'd like to make a general confession," he said. "Would you be good enough to hear me, Father?"

The priest agreed, but insisted John should go to bed first. "I'll come to your cell," he promised. "This afternoon, after Vespers."

John's confession was not a matter of minutes or even hours. It lasted three days, for Father Gonzalez interrupted it frequently to ask John additional questions about his childhood and youth. He did this at the request of the Prior, who was anxious that all details concerning the gatekeeper's life should be carefully recorded. As a result, John found himself recalling his days in Spain, his voyage to America, the two and one-half years he had worked on the ranch of Peter Jimines Menacho.

"Have you any idea of the number of souls your prayers have released from Purgatory?" inquired

"THREE TIMES SHE GAVE ME HER
LITTLE CHILD TO HOLD."

Father Gonzalez presently. "I know there must be quite a few."

The lay Brother smiled. "More than a million," he said softly. "My patron, John the Evangelist, has told me this."

The priest controlled his amazement with great difficulty. More than a million souls! What an enormous number of friends this humble lay Brother had awaiting him in Heaven!

"All right," he said calmly. "Now I want to hear about any wonder you may have kept secret till today. Think hard, Brother. Is there some grace, perhaps? Some vision?"

John's eyes were shining. "Father, three years ago Our Lady let me hold the Christ Child in my arms. I never told anyone about that."

"Three years ago? Do you remember the date, John?"

"Yes, Father. It was November 4, 1642, the feast of Saint Charles Borromeo. Ah, how happy I was then!"

"And where did this wonder take place?"

"In the Rosary chapel, Father. The statue that spoke to me during the earthquake came to life for me then. Our Lady was there before my eyes, shining like the sun. Three times she gave me her little Child to hold. It. . .it was truly wonderful!"

Presently John was relating other wonders to Father Gonzalez de Guzman. Once, while some alterations were being made about the monastery, he had come upon a carpenter who was almost in despair. The man had just sawed through a beam in the wrong place. The heavy piece of wood was far too short for its original purpose.

"And what happened, John? Did you pray about the man's mistake?"

The lay Brother nodded. "Yes, Father. You see, I knew that wood of this particular type is very hard to obtain in Peru. Besides, the poor carpenter's error would have delayed the repairs. So I knelt down on the beam..."

"Yes. Go on, John. Don't be shy about what happened."

"I knelt down on the beam and asked God to make everything right. When I got up...oh, I don't like to talk about it, Father!"

"When you got up, the beam was the correct length," said the priest calmly. "Ah, I know all about this story, John. There's no need for you to be embarrassed."

The lay Brother sighed, then slowly closed his eyes. "People say my prayers work miracles," he murmured presently, "and they thank me for helping them. But really it's God who should be thanked. It's His power that gives us what we need. Oh, if only I could make everyone understand how good He is, how kind! But I haven't the words...or the strength..."

The priest smiled. "You can tell your friends how to pray," he said gently. "You can show them how to ask God's help."

"But they know that already, Father!"

"Not all of them, John. Now, tell me. How *do* you pray?"

For a moment all was quiet in the little cell. Then a slight smile flickered on John's lips. "I just put myself in the place of a child," he said simply. "I tell the Heavenly Father of my weakness and my needs. I remind Him that His Son became man and so made Himself my Brother."

"Yes? And what else, John?"

Slowly the gatekeeper opened his eyes. "I always ask for blessings in the Name of Jesus Christ," he said softly. "That's all, Father. There's really no secret."

CHAPTER 13

FAREWELL TO THE MAGDALENA

THE DAYS PASSED, and by the middle of
September everyone realized that John
could not live much longer. He was very ill
and no medicine seemed to help. In great distress,
Father Blaise de Acosta went to the lay Brother's
cell to see what he could do. Perhaps there was
some special dish the gatekeeper would like? Or
maybe he wished to speak with one or more of his
many friends?

"No, Father Prior," said John weakly. "It's too late
for such things now. But it would please me. . .that
is, if you could arrange it. . ."

"Yes, John? What would you like?"

"To hear Mass once more, Father. That's all."

The solitary request was readily granted. The
next morning Father Blaise offered the Holy Sacrifice in John's cell, then gave him Holy Communion.
When he returned for a little visit some time later,
he found the gatekeeper lying motionless on his
hard bed. His eyes were closed and a mysterious
light seemed to be playing about his whole body.

Quickly the Prior sat down on a little bench. Surely
John had not died unattended!

"My son! Speak to me! Are you all right?"

John stirred and opened his eyes. They were
aglow with such happiness that the Prior drew back
in astonishment. "What is it?" he whispered in
awed tones. "What do you see?"

John made a little motion with his hand.
"Father. . .please don't sit just now. This room is
full of. . .of *visitors*!"

The Prior gave a quick glance around the cell.
It was empty, save for himself and the dying lay
Brother. Yet he could not doubt the latter's word.
Quickly he got to his feet, then begged for informa-
tion. Who was in the room besides themselves?

"Our Lord is here," replied John faintly. "The
Blessed Mother. . .the saints. . ."

"What saints, John?"

The gatekeeper pointed into space. Saint John
the Evangelist was present, likewise Saint Dominic,
Saint Mary Magdalen, Saints Peter and Paul, Saint
Vincent Ferrer, Saint Catherine of Siena, Saint
Louis Bertrand. . .

"Yes?" put in Father Gonzalez de Guzman, who
had just entered the room. "And who else is here?"

To the best of his ability John then described the
host of heavenly visitors gathered about his bed.
There were countless angels, also saints whose
names he did not know. All were praying for him,
bidding him not to be afraid of death.

"They are waiting to take me to Heaven," he said
simply.

"MY SON! SPEAK TO ME! ARE YOU ALL RIGHT?"

For the rest of the day the Magdalena was besieged with men and women anxious to obtain news of their beloved friend. The same question was on everyone's lips: when was the good soul going to die? Eventually the Viceroy of Peru arrived to pay his respects, in company with his son, Don Antonio de Toledo.

"We wish to ask Brother John for prayers," they told the Prior respectfully. "Do you think that he will see us?"

The Prior bowed low before the distinguished visitors. "Of course, Your Excellencies. I'll send word that you've come."

But the Viceroy hesitated a moment. "Father Prior, you know my visits have always embarrassed Brother John. He never liked compliments from anyone, much less from a man. . .well, a man high in politics and society. Perhaps, now that he's dying. . ."

Father Blaise managed a little smile, despite his sorrow at the gatekeeper's approaching death. Well he knew to what the Viceroy was referring. It concerned a visit the good man had made some time ago to thank John for a favor received through his prayers. At the time, word had gone around the Magdalena that the Viceroy wished to speak with the lay Brother and to leave him a little gift. However, no amount of searching could locate the gatekeeper. He seemed to have vanished from the face of the earth. Only later, when commanded to explain matters by the Prior, had the story come out. During the whole of the Viceroy's stay in the monastery, John had been at his accustomed post at the gate. He had seen the arrival of the Peruvian chief, the glittering assembly of noblemen and carriages, but that day God had granted his wish to remain hidden, and for several hours he had been invisible to visitors and fellow-religious alike.

"I don't think you need to worry, Your Excellencies," said the Prior reassuringly. "John knows he is going to die and praise no longer disturbs him. Last night he even said that churches are to be built in his honor."

The Viceroy stared, likewise Don Antonio. "*Churches*, Father Prior? How can that be?"

The latter shook his head. "Brother John tells us no more than this. He doesn't know when or where the churches will be built. But he insists they will come to pass. Ah, Your Excellencies, we have a real saint in our midst—one whose prophecies and miracles have been going on for years!"

The whole city of Lima agreed with the Prior. On the afternoon of September 18, the streets leading to the Magdalena were packed with huge crowds. John's prophecy that he would die that night was now general knowledge, and his devoted followers wished to come as close as they could to his deathbed. The women were in tears, for there was no possible chance that they could assist at John's passing. A rule of long standing forbade them to enter the solemn cloister of the Magdalena. However, they were well prepared to show their devotion when John's body should be brought into the public church. A number had come equipped with scissors so that they might cut off a piece of the holy Brother's habit for use as a relic. And not only the women were ready to honor the gatekeeper. Their husbands, sons and brothers carried medals and rosaries. These would be applied to John's body when the time came for it to lie in state.

As the crowd milled and surged through the streets, pressing ever closer to the main door of the monastery, one woman stood as though in a trance. This was Doña Antonia de Mejia, the wife of the merchant Peter Ramirez. Her face was twisted with grief, and from time to time she raised her arms to Heaven, then let them drop limply to her sides.

"What's the trouble?" asked a sudden voice. "Is anything wrong, Antonia?"

The woman looked up. A familiar figure was standing beside her—Gertrude de Godinez, wife of Alonso Martin de Orrelana, now Lima's leading baker. At the sight of this old friend, Doña Antonia burst into tears.

"It's my boy," she sobbed, "poor little John!"

"What about him? Is he ill, Antonia?"

The latter shook her head, and presently a most amazing story was being poured into the ears of the baker's wife. Last week, five-year-old John Ramirez had been brought to the Magdalena to see his god-father, Brother John Masias. At the time the little boy had wanted to kiss the gatekeeper's hand.

"Why, that's nothing to feel bad about!" said Gertrude gently. "Hundreds of people have done the same thing. And when your boy grows up, this will be a really precious memory."

Doña Antonia wiped her tearful eyes. "Brother John didn't want my son to kiss his hand!" she sobbed. "He said: 'It's far better for me to kiss *your* hand, little one, because very soon you are going to be an angel in Heaven.' Oh, Gertrude, I know Brother John has the gift of prophecy! And if these words mean we are going to lose our only child . . . oh, how can we bear it?"

The baker's wife was silent a moment, realizing only too well what the five-year-old youngster meant to his parents. They had waited years before God had blessed them with a child and since that happy day had always believed that the prayers of John Masias had secured the great favor.

"I wouldn't worry," she said finally. "If it really is God's will that your little boy be taken from you . . .well, wait and see if Brother John doesn't turn all your sorrow into joy."

"But he's my boy's godfather, Gertrude! Wouldn't you think . . .when he's cured so many sick people . . ."

"That he would pray for a long life for little John? Yes—I would think so, Antonia. But there must be some reason for all this and someday everything will be clear."

Then, to calm her friend's distress, Gertrude launched into a story of her own. It seemed that some time ago she had been ill with a serious fever. The only food she wanted was a dish of plums, and these were forbidden by the doctors. More than that, plums were impossible to obtain just then, for they were out of season.

"I do believe I was dying," Gertrude said firmly. "Every day I grew weaker, and finally my husband became really worried. He sent for Brother John to come and see us. The good soul arrived that very afternoon with a big basket on his arm, for he was on a begging trip for his poor. After a little visit, he told us not to worry and promised to pray for my recovery. As he was going out the door, he took a package from the basket.

" 'A little present for you,' he said. And when I opened the package, Antonia, what do you suppose was inside?"

The mother smiled, despite her heavy heart. "Some plums?"

"*Fifteen* plums!" declared Gertrude triumphantly. "Where the good soul found them, I don't know. But I ate the whole fifteen and in a few hours the fever left me. Oh, Antonia, if Brother John could be this thoughtful about a little matter of food, how much more so where your boy is concerned! Now, will you promise not to worry any more?"

Reluctantly the mother bowed her head. "I'll try," she said slowly. "My husband is with Brother John now. By this time he must have asked him to help us."

As the hours passed, many new visitors made their way to John's little cell. Among these was Father Francis de Avendaño, the priest who so often had scolded the lay Brother because of his ecstasies. Now, as he paced the corridor outside the sickroom, Father Francis twisted his hands nervously.

"I was terribly wrong," he admitted to the Prior. "Oh, Father, our John is a saint! Why didn't I realize it before?"

"It's all right," hastened Father Blaise. "Brother John says you are the only one who ever treated him as he deserved. He prays for you constantly."

Father Francis wiped away a stray tear. "I used to think he was too extreme in his penances. Sleeping on the floor, on the altar steps, fasting so often on bread and water. . .oh, the things I said to him sometimes!"

The Prior reached out a comforting hand. "Come and look at him now," he suggested. "See if he bears any grudge against you, Father."

So the two religious made their way to the little room where for the past few weeks John's life had been slowly ebbing away. They found their friend in great pain, yet still able to recognize them.

"My time. . .it isn't up yet!" he managed to gasp. "Oh, Fathers, how I long. . .for the end!"

The Prior nodded. He knew what pain John was suffering. He knew, too, that it was being offered for the salvation of sinners. Millions of men and women were too lazy and thoughtless to do penance for themselves. Well, John would do it for them. He would unite his final agony with that of Christ on the Cross. Only in the next world would the souls thus saved realize the goodness and charity of this hidden friend.

For over an hour Father Francis remained by

John's side, praying and weeping for the many unkind words he had spoken. Brother John comforted him from time to time, but towards evening his pain became so intense that he could no longer speak. Seeing this, the Prior gave the signal to commence the prayers for the dying, and soon the corridors were echoing to the sound of hurrying feet. No one wished to be absent at John's passing.

As the air filled with the ancient strains of the *Salve Regina*, that beautiful hymn sung by Dominicans whenever one of their number is dying, a little smile flickered on John's lips. His eyes, shining now with heavenly joy, turned upon Father Blaise de Acosta.

"Father, forgive me for all the trouble I've caused you," he whispered weakly. "I . . . I will try to make it up to you in Heaven."

The Prior was too overcome to reply. He fell upon his knees and took the hand of the dying lay Brother in his own.

"John . . . John . . ." he murmured.

There was not a dry eye in the little room as priests and Brothers followed their superior's example and likewise fell upon their knees. Presently there came through the window the distant voices of other friends, the men and women John had loved and who now lined the street for blocks. They were praying, too—but hardly for the gatekeeper. They were reminding God that a new saint was about to enter Heaven. In his name, and through the merits of his wonderful life, they were asking for graces for themselves and for their children.

Suddenly the bells of the Magdalena began to send their music through the gathering twilight. It was just fifteen minutes before seven o'clock. Slowly John removed his hand from that of the Prior and with a little sigh folded both arms across his breast. His eyes were closed now, his face radiant.

"Into Thy hands, O Lord, I commend my spirit!" he said softly.

The Prior leaned forward. "Brother John!" he ordered. "Look at me!"

Yet even as he spoke, Father Blaise realized the truth. No longer had John Masias an earthly superior. His faithful soul was free from bonds at last.

CHAPTER 14

AN AMERICAN HERO

IT WAS NOT until the next morning that John's body was brought to the church, but long before sunrise every available space there had been filled. Spaniards, Indians, Negroes—men and women from every walk of life—were present at the Magdalena to pay their last respects. Without doubt Lima had just given her fifth great saint to God, and there was joy in every heart at the thought.

"Remember what John said just before he died?" Father Gonzalez de Guzman asked the Prior as the two made their way into the sanctuary to look once more upon their beloved brother.

The latter nodded. "Yes, Father. I remember. John said these words: 'If it had not been for obedience, you would never have seen my face.' Well, he must be surprised now. Just look at the crowds who have come to honor him! And there are hundreds more out in the street."

Father Gonzalez gave a quick glance down the nave of the church. It presented a solid mass of people, packed into pews and standing in the aisles.

A number of children had even climbed to the window ledges, the better to observe the funeral ceremonies.

"Only a few have had a chance to touch the body," whispered the priest. "What are we going to do, Father Prior? Is the burial to be held directly after Mass?"

Father Blaise de Acosta hesitated. "That was the original plan," he said slowly, "but I'm afraid it will have to be changed. We'll have the Mass and then decide."

Presently a wave of excitement swept through the immense gathering. The Archbishop of Lima, Peter de Villagomez, was arriving with his attendants. Those who could fell at once to their knees as the prelate began to make his way up the crowded center aisle. Others were content merely to bow their heads as the Archbishop raised his hand in repeated blessing. But they lifted them quickly as a fresh commotion at the door announced the arrival of the Viceroy, attired in his magnificent robes of office and accompanied by his family and officials.

"The Archbishop and the Viceroy attend only the most important funerals," thought Brother Luis de Espina, now twenty-one years old and well on his way to completing his studies for the priesthood. "Oh, Brother John! I always knew you were a great man. Now everyone else knows it, too."

Yes—there was no doubt that Brother John was at last appreciated for the great soul he was. As Saint Dominic had fought against the heresies of thirteenth century Europe, so John had fought against the wrongs of his own day—the greed of the conquering Spaniard, the race prejudice of men in high places, the poverty and ignorance that lay upon Peru as a blight. Certainly he had never fired a gun in battle, or lifted a sword, yet he was a hero all the same—a warrior in white—whose never failing weapon was a charity that expressed itself in prayer and sacrifice for all men, everywhere. Truly Lima could be proud of this adopted son. And America could share in that righteous pride, for though John had been born in Spain he had done his most important work in the New World. He was an American saint, *an American hero,* just as much as Archbishop Turribius, Francis Solano, Rose de Flores and Martin de Porres.

As preparations for the funeral Mass got underway, Brother Luis looked once more at his dead friend. The plain cedar coffin stood in the very center of the sanctuary, in the identical spot where, seven years before, a terrified boy had fainted at the sight of a corpse. But there was no terror in Luis' eyes now. He could gaze happily on John's body, knowing that the faithful lay Brother was enjoying the beauties of Paradise.

Suddenly familiar words echoed in the ears of the young religious:

"I find it rather nice to think about the future sometimes, about the years 1724 and 1824 and so on. I ask myself if I am doing my duty now, as well as I can, so that those years will find me happy with God."

Luis started. These were the words Brother John had once spoken to six heedless boys as they played among the orange trees. Ah, what good words they had been, how full of wisdom and truth! And as he reflected upon their meaning, the young Dominican gave a deep sigh.

"I owe my vocation to you," he whispered, "and so do my friends. Dear Brother John, are you pleased that six troublesome boys are soon to be ordained? That with God's help we can look foward to eternal happiness with you?"

Half an hour passed, and the voices of the community rose and fell in the somber chant of the Requiem Mass. Finally, the Holy Sacrifice having been completed and the body blessed and incensed, the Prior made his way to the pulpit. As he did so, a hush fell upon the crowded church. What was going to happen now? Was Father Blaise going to speak about John's holy life? Above all, would he postpone the burial so that everyone could have a chance to touch the body?

There was not long to wait. Scarcely able to control his emotion, the Prior began to describe John's twenty-three years at the Magdalena and some of the wonders worked by his prayers. Presently he was telling of the marvelous powers possessed by the lay brother, powers that had enabled him to pass through locked doors, even through heavy stone walls, when called to his post by duty. Then there was the gift of vision, the reading of men's inner thoughts as though from an open book. As evidence of this latter gift, the Prior directed his words to certain mothers in the congregation.

"You have young sons here at the Magdalena," he said kindly, "and many times you have feared their health would suffer because of our many fast days. So what did you do? Whenever you laundered their habits and returned them, neatly ironed, to Brother John, you hid packages of sweets in the bundles. You knew the good soul wouldn't look inside and discover your little trick. But Brother John didn't need to look inside, my daughters. He knew all about the sweets. And your sons can tell you I speak the truth."

A murmur of astonishment ran through the listening throng, then died away as the white-clad priest continued his story. "Now I'll tell about a father," he said, "a gentleman all of you know. He has two sons at the Magdalena and because I have permission to use his name, let me give it to you. It's Captain Michael de Espina."

Once again the congregation listened to another tale of John's amazing powers. This time they learned how some years ago Captain Michael had worried about his younger boy's health. Despite the fact that the Magdalena was a house of perpetual abstinence, where no meat was eaten, he decided to bring his son a roasted chicken. This had been carefully cut up in small pieces, wrapped in paper, then placed in a basket under some apples and bananas. It was an innocent-looking gift that Captain Michael presently brought to the monastery, but Brother John was not deceived.

"Take the chicken home," he said kindly. "Don't

be responsible for making your boy break one of the important rules of the house."

The Captain obeyed, much abashed, returning later for a pleasant visit with his son. But even this extraordinary occurrence had not had a lasting effect on the goodhearted father. Some months later Captain Michael tried his little trick again, and with the same result. John knew what was hidden in the basket. It was meat, harmless and nourishing in itself, yet forbidden to the priests and Brothers of the Magdalena.

"I could tell you many other wonderful stories about our good friend," said the Prior, "but time is growing short. There's just one more thing. We have had a miracle already through John's prayers. Yes, in church at this very minute is the man concerned. He is Anthony de Alarcon, cured of his deafness last night. Ah, my friends, need I urge you to have faith in the wonderful saint all of you knew? Before you lies his body. Come now and venerate it. When everyone has had this privilege, the burial will take place in the Chapter Hall."

An exclamation of relief ran through the crowded church, and in a few minutes a vast procession was under way. Among the first to reach the body was John Lopez, a merchant recently returned from Spain. As he knelt beside the holy remains, John took the lay Brother's hand in his own, then dropped it in sudden amazement. Why, this hand was warm, like that of a living person! And there was a delightful fragrance coming from the plain cedar coffin, as of roses and lilies.

"Don't stay too long," warned Father Manuel Tamayo, once John's instructor in the liturgical rules of the Order. "Hundreds of others are waiting to pray here, too."

The merchant nodded and picked up his friend's hand again. "Dear Brother, I did what you told me to do," he whispered. "I took the money to your sister in Spain. She is well and happy and asks your prayers. I ask them, too, dear friend. Please don't forget me now that you've gone to Heaven."

As John Lopez arose from his knees, his place was quickly taken by others, a procedure that was repeated dozens of times in the next hour. Very soon Father Blaise de Acosta realized there would be no burial that day, for John's friends were too many. Quickly he sought out the Archbishop to ask permission to postpone the burial for twenty-four hours. The latter readily agreed, but there was a little smile on his face as he looked at the Prior.

"Twenty-four hours won't be long enough," he said knowingly. "After all, we have our fifth great saint in John Masias, Father Prior. There's no need to deny it, and the burial must not be held until everyone has had a chance to look at him once more. When that is to be, I leave to you."

The Prior was overjoyed that the time for John's burial had been left to his own discretion. Like everyone else, he had no desire to say good-bye to the body of the gatekeeper. Already many new cures had been reported. Cripples who had never walked were now strong and well—the result of having prayed with childlike confidence beside

John's holy remains. Blind people could see; the dumb were able to speak. As for the deaf—well, Anthony de Alarcon was only one of many cured of such an ailment.

Late that night young Brother Dionysius de Vilas made his way to the sanctuary. The church was locked now, and only a few religious were keeping watch beside the coffin. Quietly the newcomer knelt with them, the flickering funeral candles lighting up his anxious face.

"Brother John!" he whispered. "Listen to me!"

In the manner of a child seeking a favor from its father, Brother Dionysius then stated his case. An hour ago the Prior had given him some distressing news. Now that Brother John Masias had left them for Heaven, he, Brother Dionysius, was to be the keeper of the gate. He would succeed Brother John in caring for the many poor who came to the Magdalena for food and clothing.

"I've never been anything more than your assistant," sighed the young man anxiously. "Now I'm expected to take your place. Oh, how can I do this impossible thing? How can I make a few little dishes of food fill the needs of two hundred hungry people as you did?"

It was very quiet in the sanctuary, and the other priests and Brothers paid no attention to the new gatekeeper, being absorbed in their own thoughts and petitions. Realizing this, Brother Dionysius resumed his little speech with even more eloquence.

"You had so many friends, Brother John. People

in Cuzco, in Potosí, even in Spain. They helped you with alms in return for prayers. But I...I don't know anyone! Even if I did, my prayers don't work miracles and no one asks me for them. Oh, what am I going to do?"

As he prayed, Brother Dionysius was suddenly conscious of a hand placed upon his shoulder. Looking up, he saw that a familiar figure was standing beside him. It was Anthony, the Negro boy whom Brother John had saved from drowning some years back.

"Here's a letter for you, Brother," whispered the newcomer. "It must be very important because it just came by special messenger."

The new gatekeeper took the envelope Anthony handed him. It was very large and heavy, with many gold and silver seals across the back. It bore an address in Potosí, the famous mining city high in the Andes.

"I don't know anyone in Potosí," murmured the astonished lay Brother. "There must be some mistake."

Yet the writing on the envelope was plain enough. The name of Brother Dionysius de Vilas, gatekeeper of the Magdalena, was outlined in dashing black strokes.

"Gatekeeper!" cried the startled religious. "Who can know about this new work so soon?"

Aware of the sudden disturbance, the others in the sanctuary looked up from their prayers. To their amazement they saw Brother Dionysius opening an envelope from which poured a stream of banknotes.

These fell upon the floor in such quantities as to cause everyone to forget their devotions.

"What is it?" whispered one young priest anxiously. "Brother Dionysius! Who sent you all this money?"

There were tears in the lay Brother's eyes as he pointed to the coffin, to the quiet figure of his old friend. "He did it!" he choked. "Brother John has worked a miracle for *me!*"

By sunrise of the next day the remarkable story was making the rounds. This story concerned a wealthy mine owner in Potosí, one who often had helped John Masias in his charities. It seemed that some weeks ago this man had learned in a dream of the gatekeeper's approaching death. He had also learned that Brother Dionysius would be his successor and would need financial aid in caring for his poor.

"So I am sending a little donation," read the letter. *"This year has been a good one for me and I want to share what I have with others who are less fortunate. Dear Brother Dionysius, let me know whenever you need any help."*

The story of the banknotes, as well as the many cures that were taking place, served to kindle fresh devotion to John Masias. When the Archbishop, the Viceroy and another crowd of Lima's citizens arrived early that morning to attend the burial, they were informed that the ceremony had been postponed once more. It would not take place for twenty-four hours, as many people from distant towns were coming to secure relics, to touch the holy remains, to look once more upon the face of a saint.

"It's wonderful," murmured Father Gonzalez de Guzman as for the fifth time he clothed his friend's body in a fresh habit. "Why, John's prayers are working as many wonders as those of Rose and Martin. And he also needs as many new habits as they did, for people keep cutting off pieces to use as relics. Now someone has even taken one of his shoes!"

Because he feared that injury might be done to John's body by the press of the great crowds, Father Blaise de Acosta presently announced that the burial service would take place on September 21, the third day since the gatekeeper's holy death. Once again the Archbishop, the Viceroy and his officials, arrived at the Magdalena to assist at Mass. Once again every available space in church was filled, for by now all realized the truth: John Masias was really going to leave them this time. Never again would it be possible to touch his body, that body which still glowed with warmth, which filled the air with an unearthly fragrance.

"Pray for us, Brother John!" cried a woman's voice suddenly. "Help us to love God's Will!"

There was a ripple of astonishment as the woman's identity became known. She was none other than Doña Antonia de Mejía, wife of the merchant Peter Ramirez, and one not usually given to public demonstrations. But though the crowd murmured and stared, Doña Antonia did not mind. For the past three days she had been asking Brother

BL. JOHN MASIAS PRAY FOR US

JOHN MASIAS—AMERICAN SAINT,
AMERICAN HERO—PRAY FOR US!

John for a special favor. This favor was not connected with health, with success in business, with
any of the usual types of petitions John had been
granting so freely. No—Antonia's favor was a
spiritual one. She had asked for the grace to accept
willingly whatever hardships God might send her
in the future. She wanted to be a victim for sinners,
to pray and suffer for those who would not do so
for themselves.

"I was so weak," she thought, "such a coward at
the idea of losing my boy. Now—oh, Brother John!
You've changed everything! You've given me a little
of your own wonderful spirit and I'm not afraid of
God's will any more!"

Presently the immense congregation rose to its
feet, for John's body was now being carried from
the sanctuary to its last resting place in the Chapter
Hall of the monastery. Doña Antonia also rose—her
eyes shining, her heart filled with a wonderful
peace. How splendid it was to be alive, to know that
even the weakest soul can do good for others if only
it asks God's help!

"I'm not afraid of sorrow now," she whispered,
"even if it does mean losing my little boy. I accept
God's will with all my heart. I embrace it. Oh,
Brother John—*thank you!*"

New York City
Feast of Saint Agnes of Montepulciano
April 20, 1944

More books by the same author . . .

<u>8 MORE</u> GREAT CATHOLIC
BOOKS FOR CHILDREN
. . . and for all young people ages 10 to 100!!

1230 SAINT PAUL THE APOSTLE—The Story of the Apostle to the Gentiles. 231 pp. PB. 23 Illus. Impr. The many adventures that met St. Paul in the early Catholic Church.   13.00

1231 SAINT BENEDICT—The Story of the Father of the Western Monks. 158 pp. PB. 19 Illus. Impr. The life and great miracles of the man who planted monastic life in Europe.   8.00

1232 SAINT MARGARET MARY—And the Promises of the Sacred Heart of Jesus. 224 pp. PB. 21 Illus. Impr. The wonderful story of remarkable gifts from Heaven. Includes St. Claude de la Colombière.   11.00

1233 SAINT DOMINIC—Preacher of the Rosary and Founder of the Dominican Order. 156 pp. PB. 19 Illus. Impr. The miracles, trials and travels of one of the Church's most famous saints.   8.00

Continued on next page . . .

At your Bookdealer or direct from the Publisher.
Call Toll Free 1-800-437-5876

1234 KING DAVID AND HIS SONGS—A Story of the Psalms. 138 pp. PB. 23 Illus. Impr. The story of the shepherd boy who became a warrior, a hero, a fugitive, a king, and more. 8.00

1235 SAINT FRANCIS SOLANO—Wonder-Worker of the New World and Apostle of Argentina and Peru. 205 pp. PB. 19 Illus. Impr. The story of St. Francis' remarkable deeds in Spain and South America. 11.00

1236 SAINT JOHN MASIAS—Marvelous Dominican Gatekeeper of Lima, Peru. 156 pp. PB. 14 Illus. Impr. The humble brother who fought the devil and freed a million souls from Purgatory. 8.00

1237 BLESSED MARIE OF NEW FRANCE—The Story of the First Missionary Sisters in Canada. 152 pp. PB. 18 Illus. Impr. The story of a wife, mother and nun—and her many adventures in pioneer Canada. 9.00

1238 ALL 8 BOOKS ABOVE (Reg. 76.00)   THE SET: 60.00

Prices subject to change.

MARY FABYAN WINDEATT

Mary Fabyan Windeatt could well be called the "storyteller of the saints," for such indeed she was. And she had a singular talent for bringing out doctrinal truths in her stories, so that without even realizing it, young readers would see the Catholic catechism come to life in the lives of the saints.

Mary Fabyan Windeatt wrote at least 21 books for children, plus the text of about 28 Catholic story coloring books. At one time there were over 175,000 copies of her books on the saints in circulation. She contributed a regular "Children's Page" to the monthly Dominican magazine, *The Torch*.

Miss Windeatt began her career of writing for the Catholic press around age 24. After graduating from San Diego State College in 1934, she had gone to New York looking for work in advertising. Not finding any, she sent a story to a Catholic magazine. It was accepted—and she continued to write. Eventually Miss Windeatt wrote for 33 magazines, contributing verse, articles, book reviews and short stories.

Having been born in 1910 in Regina, Saskatchewan, Canada, Mary Fabyan Windeatt received the Licentiate of Music degree from Mount Saint Vincent College in Halifax, Nova Scotia at age 17. With her family she moved to San Diego in that same year, 1927. In 1940 Miss Windeatt received an A.M. degree from Columbia University. Later, she lived with her mother near St. Meinrad's Abbey, St. Meinrad, Indiana. Mary Fabyan Windeatt died on November 20, 1979.

(Much of the above information is from Catholic Authors: Contemporary Biographical Sketches 1930-1947, *ed. by Matthew Hoehn, O.S.B., B.L.S., St. Mary's Abbey, Newark, N.J., 1957.)*